How Short Hitting, Bad Golfers Break 90 All the Time

Fred Fields
Illustrated by Stephen Stanton

TABLE OF CONTENTS

INTRODUCTION

The secret to playing good golf is not playing like a pro. Touring golf pros are young, healthy, and talented, and practice 8 to 12 hours every day, rain or shine. They hit anywhere from 400 to 1,000 practice balls every day, depending on who you listen to.

They hit 300 yard drives right down the middle of very narrow fairways. They hit 200 yard 6 iron shots over a pond to within 8 feet of the hole.

And yet, often, they don't shoot par or better.

If they're so talented, and they work so hard, and they can't break par every time, maybe you should be mindful of that when setting your sights on your golfing goal. Because, you're probably never going to be a professional golfer; and you're never going to play like a professional golfer.

So you should learn to adjust your shot making to golf shots you can perform, and not try to do what is beyond your capability.

By that I mean, if you will make a small effort to improve your ball striking, and learn to think your way around the course, you can be scoring 20 shots better a round. And, if you really try to improve, you can be scoring in the low 80's or even the high 70's within a reasonable time.

Understand this. Your local pro will try to teach you how to hit a golf ball, but he makes no effort to teach you how to play the game.

Secondly, most golfers are lucky to play once or twice a week, and they never practice. A business-man, who isn't paid to play the game, and who rarely plays, and who never practices, can't expect to hit golf shots like a pro.

Finally, most golfers don't know how to think on a golf course. My pappy used to say, "It always amazes me that a golfer who can't hit a fairway 50 yards wide, thinks he can hit the ball between two trees 18 inches apart"

When I say "think on a golf course", I don't mean thinking about hitting the ball. I'm talking about "strat-egizing" about how to defeat the golf course, or more correctly, how to keep the golf course from defeating you. Because, in golf, you have only one opponent, the course, and, overwhelmingly, more than 99.99% of the time, the course wins.

On Monday morning, check the PGA tourna-ment scores. Some weeks, less than half of the pros break par. Some weeks, **none** of them break par. Hale Irwin won his first US Open Championship with a score of 7 OVER PAR!

I am not a golf pro. I am a teacher. I am 71 years old, can't hit a drive over 180 yards (or about as far as Tiger Woods hits an 8 iron) but last year, when I was 70, I shot a 76. Not my age, but pretty darned close.

When I was young and strong, my typical drive went 225 to 230 yards, and I often played from the back tees on a course that was 7200 yards long. My best score from those back tees was 73. Now I'm old and sick and weak, but, just by knowing how to think on a golf course, I regularly play in the 80's, sometimes in the 70's (but not often any more).

I've been playing since Pappy bought me a set of clubs for my 14th birthday. And over the years, I've taken a lot of lessons, hit a lot of balls, and got a lot of tips. Most of you have been down the same road, but probably not for as many years. What I'm going to teach you in this book will take 20 strokes a round off your game, even if you don't change your grip, stance or swing.

But if you read this book, and make a few intelligent adjustments to your swing and grip and stance, you'll learn why your current game is unacceptable, what you're doing wrong, and how to make corrections. And you'll always play under 90, and if you really try, sometimes under 80.

CHAPTER 1: THE THEORY OF GOLF

Golf, even for the great golfers, is an exasperating game. It should be so simple. After all, the ball is just sitting there waiting to be hit. No one is throwing you a curve ball, like in baseball. No one is trying to keep you from your goal, like in basketball or hockey. No one is knocking you down to keep you from doing what you want to do, like in football. So why is it so tough?

First of all, the ball is pretty small. And the hitting surface of the golf club is not much bigger. And it really is several games in one…hitting long drives, hitting partial shots to a small target, then putting the ball into an even smaller hole. Mainly it's tough because most golfers have no idea, really, of how to play the game.

So, let's start at the beginning. Golf is a game of distance and direction. It's not how far **can** you hit the ball, it's how far **will** you hit the ball, and in what direction.

***

Imagine a circle. On the bottom of the circle is a small dot. And another small dot is at the center of the circle. In your mind, draw a straight line, connecting the dots.

The circle represents the path of the golf club-head.

(Have you ever seen the Iron Byron machine hit a ball? Look up Iron Byron on the internet. You'll see. The clubhead travels pretty much in a circle, all in one plane.)

The dot at the bottom of the circle represents the golf ball.

The dot in the center represents the golfer's head.

And the line connecting the dots represents the golfer's front arm and the shaft of the golf club. (Since both lefties and righties will read this book, I'm going to refer to "front and back sides", rather than "left and right sides". Your front side, is the side closest to your target. Your back side is the side farthest from your target.)

In theory, the clubhead starts at the ball, travels back along the circumference of the circle. Then it returns to and through the ball, back along the same circular path.

If you move the center of the circle, the circle moves the same. Center up, circle up...top the ball. Center back, away from its original position, the circle moves back, and the club head hits behind the ball.

So, the ideal swing includes **not** moving your head: up, down, or sideways. Check the swing pictures of the professional golfers' swings in the magazines.

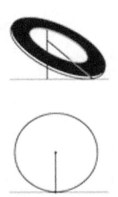

CAPTION: 3 dimensional picture of the swing circle above the swing circle.

These two drawings represent the perfect golf swing. One is the circle just described. The other, which looks like a tether ball pole, represents the swing circle tilted, as we golfers use it. A perfect swing will swing the club in a tilted circle all in one plane, as in that drawing

***

While we're talking about rightys and leftys, I want to tell you a story about two friends of mine, Larry, a right-handed 2 handicapper who is a long hitter, and Rob, a left-handed 6 handicapper who hits the ball short. (This incident happened over 30 years ago, when 260 yards was a pretty long drive.)

One day, Rob and Larry were out of town, and having finished their business, they met up at the local municipal course. Playing on about the 7th hole, they caught up with a foursome of old duffers who waited for them on the tee and allowed them to play through.

Rob had the honors, and hit his usual 230 yard drive, left handed, right down the middle. The old duffers were impressed, wishing that they could play like Rob.

Then Larry stepped up, and topped Rob by hitting his ball 265, right handed, also down the middle. Of course, the old duffers were even more impressed... and said so, enthusiastically!

As he picked up his bag and started to leave the tee, responding to the duffers' comments on Larry's better shot, Rob said, "You notice, he makes me play left-handed!"

***

Now back to the theory. Golf is a sport, played by athletes. There is a magic athletic move in most sports...golf, tennis, baseball, track, boxing, football, etc. Imagine that your spine and shoulders form a letter "T". The magic move is the rotation of the shoulders around the spine. Stand up; put both hands on your chest. Now, holding your head in the same place, rotate your shoulders back and forth. That's the "magic move".

It is the move a pitcher makes in baseball, or a quarterback in football, when he throws a ball.

It is the move a tennis player makes when he hits the ball.

It is the move a boxer makes when he throws a punch...the rotation of the shoulders around the spine.

That is the move a good golfer makes when he hits a golf shot. He rotates his shoulders around the base created by his spine, and topped by his head. In a good golf shot, the head and spine stay still until after the ball is hit, and the shoulders move the arms and hands through the ball.

The most obvious difference between a good golfer's swing and a not good golfer's swing, is the shoulder movement. On all his shots, from the long drive, to the short putt, the good golfer rotates his shoulders around his spine, while keeping his head still. He makes the magic move.

But there's more. Watch a pitcher, a quarter-back, or a boxer make the magic move. As he does, he transfers his weight from his back foot to his front foot, gaining additional momentum and power. The same rule applies to the golf swing.

On the backswing, transfer your weight to your back foot. Then, as you swing into the ball, transfer your weight to your front foot. **But keep your head and spine in the same place.**

That is the basic swing; for every shot, from the longest drive to the shortest putt. The only difference between driving and putting is the distance you move the clubhead along the circle. The easy thing about golf, is that you only have to learn one swing.

In this book, I'll teach you how to master that one swing, starting with the easiest stroke, the short putt, and on up to the longest drive.

Well, actually, the easiest shot in golf, after the practice swing and the 'gimmie putt' is the greenside sand shot...you don't even have to hit the ball.

***

But even more important than hitting the golf ball, to score well on a golf course, you must learn how to "outthink" the golf course. There is a lot more to playing the game than hitting the ball.

If every shot were perfect, the golfer could just walk around the course hitting the ball and birdying every hole. But they're not all perfect. In fact, if you hit even one perfect shot per round, you're doing well. You must know how to avoid unnecessary problems on the course, and how to react when problems arise. That's playing the game, and that's what this book is all about. If you just knew how to think on a golf course, you'd always break 90.

CHAPTER 2: THE GRIP

One thing the pros have right, is that every golf lesson or book begins with the grip.

The grip truly is the key to a good swing. A good grip will tell you where your club head is facing at any time. It will keep a mis-hit shot on line. It will allow you to take a firm grip on the shaft of the club, and still swing relaxed.

The first step in understanding the grip is to put your two hands together, palm to palm, fingers extended, like in a "praying" pose. This is the correct relationship of the hands in the perfect grip...both hands with palms on opposite sides of the same plane.

Now, move your hands, still in the praying position, back and forth, like swinging a gate, with your wrists being the gate hinge. This is the correct "wrist action" in the swing. When Ben Hogan revealed his secret move, "cup the left wrist" that is what he meant. The correct wrist action cocks the wrists away from the target on the backswing, and "uncocks" the wrists as they swing through the ball toward the target. Coming from the top of your backswing to impact with the ball, your wrists should "close the gate". That means, they must be perpendicular to the line of the ball's flight at impact.

(I was teaching a lady this wrist action, and she couldn't picture the "closing the gate", so I gave her an alternate swing picture. Imagine you are paddling a child with a paddle. The timing and the wrist action are exactly like that. She knew what I was trying to say. She had a lot of paddling experience with her three sons.

***

Before we talk about the grip, let's talk a little bit about your muscles. Place one hand on your other forearm. Now, with the free hand make a fist, and feel the muscles in your arm that contract when you make the fist. Open your hand, and now, flex your fingers like a claw. Notice that entirely different muscles contract to form the claw than to form the fist. The muscles you use in the proper golf grip are the "claw" muscles, because you grip the club with your fingers, (your "claws").

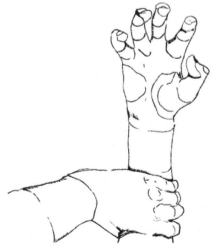

CAPTION: Hand on forearm with fingers clenched in a "claw".

That's some of the muscles that come into play. Now open your back side hand (right hand for right-handers), fingers out straight, palm up. Move your thumb inward toward your fingers. This will cause a mushy bulb of muscle at the base of the thumb to show up. The **top** of your front side (other hand) thumb fits neatly into that bulb at the thumb base to weld the hands together in the proper golf grip. Put it there.

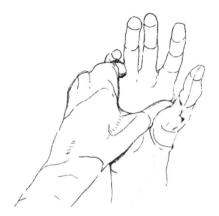

CAPTION: Left thumb pressed into the bulb of muscle at the base of the right thumb. Notice the index finger/"pinkie" connection.

Now, interlock or overlap your pinkie and index fingers (whichever is most comfortable for you), then curl your remaining fingers around an imaginary golf shaft. Notice that your palms are on the opposite sides of the same plane. This is the perfect golf grip. Notice how the hands are "welded" together at the thumbs and at the pinkie-index finger connection.

Next, let's insert the shaft of the club into that perfect grip. As a practical matter, your front side hand goes on the grip first. Put the club's grip in your front side hand, laying it across the palm from the heel of the palm, crossing the base of the index finger. The palm of the front side hand is the foundation for your grip **And that front side palm must be on the same plane as the leading edge of the club face.** Curl the last three fingers of that hand around the club, and lay that thumb on the top of the club shaft. Do not extend that thumb or that wrist. The club is controlled with those last three fingers (claws).

CAPTION: Position of the grip in the left hand (Right-handers)

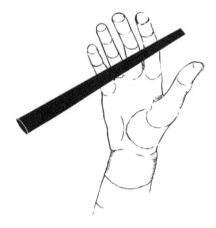

CAPTION: Position of the grip in the right hand (Right-handers)

Finally, with the back side hand, overlap or inter-lock the pinkie with the index finger of the front side hand; curl the two middle fingers around the shaft, **keeping the shaft of the club gripped in <u>the fingers and keeping the backside palm off the grip</u>**. Cover the front side thumb with the bulb at the base of the back side thumb, and lay the thumb straight down the shaft, just across the centerline of the shaft. Finally, the back-side index finger should be gently wrapped around the grip, not exerting any force onto the club. The two middle fingers (claws) of the backside hand control the club.

About counting knuckles, or direction of the "V's", <u>forget that</u>! Your palms must be on the same plane, and that plane must be the plane of the face of the club. That is the plane created by the **leading edge** of the club face. And the strength of the grip must be in your fingers, using the claw muscles described above. On mis-hit shots, these fingers will keep your clubface straight and perpendicular to your ball's line of flight.

Grab a paddle or a tennis racket (or imagine grabbing one as I taught the lady above). Your natural grip will put your palm on the same plane as the face of the racket or paddle. In which case, you will instinctively know the direction the paddle or racket is facing. Well, the same is true with the direction the golf club's face is pointing...**the same direction as the palm of your back side hand!**

CAPTION: This picture, although not showing the correct position of the hand in the grip, shows the palm of the right hand on the same plane as the leading edge of the golf club.

It is important to know where your club is facing when you hit a shot, because the face of the club controls which direction your ball will start out...hopefully, straight toward your target! And with the proper grip, you always know.

I know this was a bit complicated. I promise to make the rest of the book less so.

One more thing about the grip...the reason you interlock or overlap your fingers and weld the thumbs together, forming a single unit with the two hands.

In the early years of major league baseball, there was a Hall of Fame player named Wee Willie Keeler. Wee Willie was small, and not a home run slugger. His value, as with Pete Rose, was that he got a lot of singles and doubles by, as he said it, "Hitting them where they ain't". Willie's grip had his hands spread apart with a gap of about an inch between them, so he could spray hits all over the ball park.

Well, in golf, we don't want to spray hits all over the park. We want to hit them on a straight line, down the middle of the fairway, every time. So, we interlock our fingers and weld our thumbs together to make our hands work together as a single unit.

CHAPTER 3: PUTTING

We start with putting the ball because it is the shortest use of the clubhead circle, the easiest shot to learn, the easiest to improve, and **_the most important shot in a round of golf_**. Remember, a one inch putt counts one stroke, the same as a 300 yard drive. Of a standard 72 strokes to par, it is planned that exactly ½, or 36, will be putts.

"Good putting can overcome bad driving. But nothing can overcome bad putting." (Pappy)

Most golf courses are par 72, or at least most golf course architects plan for them to be par 72. They just don't always turn out that way. Let's think about that. 18 holes, times 4 strokes, including two putts, on every hole, equals par 72. What if par on every hole was 5? 18 holes times 5 strokes, 2 of them putts, equals 90 strokes.

Our goal is 90 strokes or better. So, if you can 2 putt every hole, with three shots to every green, even the par 3's, that's 90 strokes. Or, put another way, score 5 on every hole, with a 4 on one par 3, and you've broken 90! You see how important putting is? The first step to breaking 90 is...**no more than two putts per green!**

And which is the easiest shot to improve? The shortest stroke, the putt.

"Ah!" you say, "but what about the par 5's?" Good question. Par on them is three shots to the green, plus two putts. Ask any pro or low handicapper. No! Ask **every** pro or low handicapper, they will tell you that the **easiest holes to par are the par 5's.** On the par 5's the course lets you miss a shot, and still make a par. In a professional golf tournament, the pros figure that if you bogie a par five, you've given away two strokes to the field. They expect to birdie par fives.

As your ball striking improves, you'll see that I'm right. But if the par fives are an issue, figure that bogie, one over the scorecard par, is par for you. That's still 90 strokes...4 on par 3's; 5 on par 4's; and 6 on par 5's. It still comes out 90, and still, one par in 18 holes breaks 90.

So, the first change in your thinking on a golf course should be...on the green in three, and two putts. Put the ball <u>ANYWHERE ON THE GREEN</u> in three shots, and two putt.

This being the case, **your goal on first putts is not to make those 15 and 20 foot putts; only to put the ball close enough to the hole to make your second putt automatic.**

Think about this. You have a 20 foot putt. What are the odds of you making that putt? One in ten? Maybe? What are the odds of you making it in two putts if you are trying to make it in two putts? Maybe nine in ten.

So you see, the odds are the same both ways. It's just easier going for it in two putts. And you're less likely to hit that first putt badly, causing a 3-putt.

We're trying to break 90. Two putts is our goal. It costs us nothing if we don't sink the first putt. There's no pressure. Just try to put it close to the hole. Take a quick look at the general slope of the green; are you putting uphill or downhill; will the putt break left or right; and how hard should you hit it in the general direction of the hole? Then, with no pressure, putt it close to the hole.

Remember, I said golf is a game of distance and direction. No place is it more obvious than on the green.

And distance is a lot more important than direction on the green. When you miss a putt directionally, you usually miss by a foot or two. When you miss by distance, you may putt the ball clear off the green!

Remember, two putts per green, and distance is paramount!

With that in mind, let's talk about how to putt.

Let's go back to the circle of the swing. In putting, we only use about two feet at the bottom of the circle. The keys are, **keep your head still,** keep the putter head close to the ground, and make your stroke straight back, away from the hole along the line of the putt, and accelerate straight through the ball along the line of the putt.

You putt with your shoulders...the magic move. The reason is that, anatomically, the shoulders will stay online if rotated. Also, the shoulders are easier to hit through the ball, not stopping at impact, which is supremely important. The hands, arms, and wrists, combined, will move in infinite directions. So the putt must be driven by the shoulders.

Again, turn on the TV, watch the pros do it. They use the magic move on every putt. They hit the ball with their shoulders. Most **use no wrist action at all** and, on this shot, they do not shift their weight...they keep it solidly in one place. Here, the extra power of the weight shift is not needed. This is not a power shot, it is a total finesse shot.

The pros use all kinds of putters and all kinds of grips. But they all started with the standard putter and the regular golf grip. The reason some changed is because they had problems. Every golfer you see with a long putter, or a weird grip, had problems putting at some time in his career, and had to search for a cure. But they all started with the standard golf grip, and the standard golf putter.

Here's how to putt. Stand up to the ball with your feet a comfortable distance apart. For me, I like my feet close together, as with Raymond Floyd's stance, because that cuts down on the ball location errors. (Your putting stroke changes if the ball is too far forward or too far back in your setup.)

The ball should be about in the middle of your stance. Relax and bend over from the waist. Using the shoulders only, swing the putter back a short distance, then accelerate the club head through the ball toward the hole. If you have trouble feeling the proper move, concentrate on your front shoulder (left shoulder for righties) on the backswing, and to further guarantee the proper use of the shoulders on the putt, press your back elbow (right elbow for righties) in against your body. This will insure the proper use of the shoulders, coordinate your body and shoulder turn, and help to keep your club head on the line of the putt.

How far you backswing away from the ball depends on how far you are from the hole. Short distance, short backswing. Long distance, longer backswing. The main thing is that the stroke must be smooth with no extra jabs to hit the ball harder. If you need to hit the ball farther, take a little bit longer backswing on your putt.

Always follow through! This is extremely important, especially on short putts. The follow-through on short putts keeps your clubhead on the line of the putt, making sure that you hit the ball on the right line. Too often on short putts, players try to POP the ball into the hole...not good. Stroke the ball into the hole, and to guarantee this, always use a long follow through. I once went six months without missing a 3 foot putt. The secret was an exaggerated follow through.

DO'S AND DON'T'S OF PUTTING
- **Keep your head still!**(Especially don't move it forward as you putt.)
- Do not transfer weight, like in a longer swing

- Light but firm grip of the club. Imagine you're holding an open tube of toothpaste and you don't want to squeeze out any paste.
- Swing straight back and straight through along the line of the putt, keeping the putter head close to the ground.* Keeping your head immobile, use only your shoulders (the magic move) and keep your back side elbow and upper arm in against your body.
- Accelerate your putter through the ball
- Follow through, straight down the line of the putt...even exaggerate the follow through. It will help you hit the ball straight toward the hole.
- Accelerate through the ball
- Again...accelerate through the ball. The most common error in putting...especially short putting, is deceleration of the club head during the swing into the ball. (in fact, on **all** shots, **_acceleration is a very important key_** to the golf swing.)

    * Backswing in putting is critical, and often overlooked. The backswing should be 180 degrees straight back, along the line of the putt, followed by a stroke forward, through the ball, along the same line. Don't bring the club head back inside the line of the putt, and swing "around" your body. It must be straight back and straight through, in a straight line along the line of the putt.

    A great golf practice tool is two short boards, about 30" long, 2 x 4's or 1 x 4's, and a tin can, about the size (4" across) of a golf hole, with the top and bottom cut out of the can. On your carpet or a rug at home, lay the two boards parallel to each other, a little bit farther apart than the length of your putter head. Then lay the tin can on its side, about 5 to 7 feet away. Lay a ball near the center of the boards, then, keeping the putter head between the boards, try to putt the ball past the boards, stopping it inside the can.

***

At the golf course, before teeing off, go to the putting green with a putter and 3 balls. Find two holes about 25 feet apart. Putt the balls back and forth between the two holes a few times, trying to stop the balls close to the target hole, so that you have a feel for how hard to hit the putts to make them go 25 or so feet. Don't try to sink the practice putts, **just get them close to the hole**. Long or short doesn't matter, just close matters. If one hole is uphill of the other, even better...you'll get a feel for putting uphill and downhill.

Remember! It's important not to worry about sinking those practice putts. Your goal is to "feel" the distance, and how hard to hit the ball. Don't worry about direction...distance only!

When you're on the course, you'll have a feel for those 25 foot putts, and your brain will estimate how hard to hit a 20, 30, 40 foot or longer putt.

Next, on the putting green, take your balls 2 to 6 feet from the hole. Now, practice sinking those putts. Try 2 feet; then 3 feet; then 4 feet, and so on, until you have a feel for putting those short putts on line into the hole. And remember, head still, accelerate, and exaggerate your follow-through.

<u>Here's an important fact that few golfers realize</u>: Your brain is a computer. (Ever hear a computer called a Mechanical Brain?) It accepts, processes, and gives back information. I'm going to refer to this several times throughout the book. Your brain is a computer. Be aware of the data you are entering into it, and retrieve the data as you need it...like how hard to hit a putt. After you've hit 8 or 10 of those 25 foot putts, your computer brain has stored the information, and will send that information to your body to retrieve as needed. (Just as when you were a child, you "stored" the multiplication tables, and now can retrieve them as needed.)

On very long putts, to get a feel for how hard to hit the ball, go to a spot approximately ½ way between your ball and the hole. Imagine hitting a ball to the hole from that distance. Take a few practice swings. Input that memory into your brain and muscles. Then, immediately go back to the ball. Take one or two practice swings, swinging twice as hard as the halfway swings. Then, before you forget, step up, settle yourself, and putt.

***

Reading putts, deciding which way the ball will break, and how hard to hit the ball is an art easily learned.

To "read" putts during your round of golf:
- First note if the putt is uphill, downhill, or level, or a combination of several.

- Next, stand behind the ball and check the general slope of the green...right, left, or level.
- Finally, while standing behind your ball, and **starting at the hole**, read the line of the putt back from the hole to your ball.
- As you read the line of the putt, find the spot near the hole where, when the putt loses its momentum, it will fall into the hole. Then putt to stop the ball's momentum at that spot.
- Remember, your goal is to put the ball close to the hole with the first putt, and to have a no-brainer left for your second putt. You are not trying to sink that first putt unless it is within 6 feet of the hole.

Let's talk a minute about momentum. Any rock will fly, as long as it's thrown hard enough, and travels fast enough. It falls to earth when it slows down and loses its momentum. I can't understand why a golfer will hit a putt five feet past the hole and say, "It didn't break". When, after losing its momentum, it broke **2 feet!** Most putts go straight until they lose their momentum. The secret of putting is to figure out how far the putt will break **after it loses its momentum**, and how hard to hit it to get it to the right spot for it to begin slowing down.

Your job on the putting green is to figure how hard to hit the ball and what spot to hit it to, to get it to fall into the hole, just before it stops rolling. And the ball will travel straight to that spot until its momentum is slowed, so, you don't have to allow for break from where the ball sits until it reaches that momentum stopping spot.

Former US Open champion Hubert Green said, "95% of putts that are short don't go in." Well, 95% of putts that go past the hole don't go in either.

Don't worry about short or long. Just worry about too short or too long. Just try to putt the ball within a foot or two of the cup, so that the second putt is a tap in.

Sometimes, you can't tell if a ball will break right or left.

Pappy says. "If you can't tell which way a putt will break, putt it straight at the hole. That way, no matter which way it breaks, it won't go in." But if it's well struck, it won't be far away either.

Remember, first putts close to the hole...second putts in the hole.

Here's a tip about finding the line of a putt. It's easier to see the break of a putt looking uphill than looking downhill. If you have a downhill putt, go down behind the hole and look back up at the ball. The right or left break will show itself better when you're looking uphill. And, as you're walking around the green, check the slopes. Sometimes, the slope will reveal itself when looking from a certain direction. That's why Tiger Woods walks a circle around his putts, to check and recheck the breaks from every direction.

If you really want to know how important putting is, remember Billy Casper. Billy wasn't a great striker of the ball. He wasn't a long ball hitter. He didn't have the best long irons. But he was known as the best putter on tour for about 20 years. In that time, he won 51 tournaments, including the US Open (twice) and the Masters. (Only Sam Snead, Ben Hogan, Jack Nicklaus, Arnold Palmer, Byron Nelson, and Tiger Woods have won more...and that's pretty good company!) Billy Casper is proof that putting is critical.

So, take the pressure off. Just remember that that 30 foot putt is successful if it ends up close to the hole. The pressure begins if you leave that first putt 10 feet from the hole. **Because we need to have no more than 2 putts per hole.**

Another word about two putts per hole. Every now and then, even the worst player hits two lucky shots, and winds up lying 2, about 12 feet from the hole. All of a sudden, he is thinking BIRDIE!!!! **WRONG!** Half the time, trying to sink that birdie putt, he hits the ball 5 feet past the hole, misses the come-backer, and winds up with a bogey or worse. Remember, for the guy trying to break 90, **bogey is his par**! If he makes a par, that's a birdie for him. Make sure that, if the first putt doesn't go in, the second one is a gimmee! <u>**Save that par**</u>!

Here are a couple of games you can play on the putting green to improve your putting.

<u>GAME NUMBER 1: AROUND THE WORLD</u>—Take six balls, put them in a circle around a hole, with each ball 2 feet from the hole. Then sink the putts. Then do it from 3 feet, 4 feet, and 5 feet. The reason for the game is to get you used to sinking putts going uphill, down-

hill, breaking right, and breaking left. And to be able to do it from these distances, so that you'll be confident sinking those second putts when you leave them more than tap in distance from the hole.

GAME NUMBER 2: SOLITAIRE—(And just as with cards, it's tough to beat this game.) Take 5 balls and 4 tees to the putting green. Go to a hole, and lay out the course.

To lay out the course, lay your putter on the ground with the head at the hole, and the grip away from the hole, about 3 feet. (Most standard putters are almost three feet long). Mark the end of the putter by sticking a tee in the green. We'll call that a 3 foot putt. Now lay the putter down again, sticking a tee at the end, approximately 6 feet from the cup. Finally, guesstimate 4 feet and 5 feet between the 3 foot and 6 foot tees. You now have locations to practice 3 foot, 4 foot, 5 foot, and 6 foot putts along the same line.

CAPTION: Setting up the course for Solitaire.

The game is: from 3 feet, sink 5 straight putts or 9 of 10. Once you succeed at this, go to 4 feet: again, 5 in a row, or 9 of 10. Then do the same from 5 feet and 6 feet, except for those lengths, it's 8 of 10, or 5 in a row. But here's the kicker...if you miss at 4, 5, or 6 feet, you start all over again at 3 feet. Try not to leave the green until you've completed all four stations on the course. I'd say that I've beat this game, maybe one in 20 times...but I've sure improved my 3, 4, 5, and 6 foot putting. The real genius of this game is that the pressure mounts as you get closer to winning, so it's not like standing on the driving range and missing a shot. Here, there are consequences for missing!

Finally, putting is a very individual pursuit. What works for me, may not work for you. The way I putt has evolved over 57 years of trial and error. The basics are the same. The goals are the same. But the individual methods are different.

What I'm trying to say is, experiment. Experiment with your grip. Try choking down on the club. Experiment with your stance, does it work better open, closed or square? Experiment with the placement of the ball, off the front toe, off the back toe, or in the middle of your stance? Do you putt better bent over or more upright? Close to the ball, or farther away? Tighter grip or looser grip?

The main thing is to get the ball close to the hole on the long putts, and to have a reasonably good chance to make those within 6 feet of the hole.

CHAPTER 4: CHIPPING

After putting, the next easiest stroke, and the next easiest stroke to perfect, is chipping, defined as hitting the ball onto the green from just off the green. This shot, when you get good at it, is a real stroke saver.

It has been said that, "It's not how, it's how many." On in 3, and one putt, is par, just like on in 2 and two putts. So, if you can hit the ball close to the green in 2, then chip close for a one-putt green, you can save a lot of pars. That's how the pros do it.

And here's a tip. I already told you I was a short hitter, even when I was young and strong. When betting against a long hitter who had a handicap equal to or better than mine, I found that being a short hitter was often an advantage. On many holes, the long hitter would be on the green in regulation and I'd be just off. He'd figure he had a win, expecting a two putt for himself, and a chip and two putts for me. But I'd chip up close and one putt, making him two putt for the half. After a bunch of these, his attitude would be, "What do I have to do the beat this guy?"

Now, about chipping. Most pros recommend low pitched, 6 or 7 irons from close to the green, and higher pitched from farther away. Their reasoning is that you should drop the ball on the green, close to the edge, and let it roll to the hole, rather than flying the ball to the hole. (The exception being if you have to clear a bunker or water, or bad ground of any kind, or uneven ground, then you use a higher pitched wedge and make sure you clear the hazard.)

I can't hit anything farther than 175 yards, so my short game is pretty much limited to a 9 iron, which I use from 75 yards in, or a sand wedge, which I use to hit over obstacles. Even on the short chips, I use a 9 iron. It's ok for a pro, who practices every day to use different clubs for different chips, but for me, I use the same 9 iron for all of them. I only have time to practice with one club...not several. You might like to try a 6 or 7 or 8 iron, and see what is the most comfortable for you.

Also, I find that I am more focused on the line of chips than I am on the line of long putts. A good chipper should be able to hit the ball on any line he chooses. So, I concentrate on trying to figure how the ball will break, and I try to hit the ball an appropriate distance. **That 76 I shot last year was the result of a uniquely good day chipping and pitching close for one-putt greens**.

Now comes the question, how do you hit this shot? It's really quite simple, because the chip shot is little more than an extension of the putt.

For chip shots, **choke down on the club**, address the ball with your **hands ahead of the ball**, in other words, your wrists should already be cocked a little. Right elbow in against your body (right-handers). Concentrate your weight mostly on your front foot. Keep your head still. And remember the magic move...only use your shoulders on this shot. No hands, no wrists, no weight transfer **and don't move your head**. Just turn your shoulders away from the target, then turn back. And remember, **always accelerate through the shot!** Never decelerate into the ball. Take a seriously short backswing if you must, but accelerate through the shot! And follow through. Do **not** stop at the ball. Your follow through is to allow you to accelerate until after you hit the ball, then slow down only after the ball has taken off.

Many pros suggest that you open your stance a little bit on the chip. I have done it with an open stance and with a square stance. Both work. Try them both in practice, and use whichever works best for you. (Open stance means, that a line from your back toe, past your front toe, continues on a line, if you're right handed, to the left of your target. Your front shoulder is also pulled away from your target line.)

DO'S AND DON'T'S OF CHIPPING

- Feet closer together at address, and try opening your stance. Most of your weight on your front foot.
- Flex your knees and bend over at the waist.
- Choke down on the club and get your hands ahead of the ball by starting your wrist cock while still at the address position.
- Right elbow in against your body
- Rotate your shoulders back in a short back-swing, **keeping the backswing flat, close to the ground.**
- Pause at the top of the backswing, then accelerate the clubhead into and through the ball with a generally downward motion until

you have hit the ball. The club head should hit the ground <u>lightly</u> **after** you have hit the ball.

- Follow through.

CAPTION: When chipping, keep the backswing short and close to the ground. And follow through.

It is a good idea to take a narrower stance, with your feet closer together than on longer shots, and take a couple of practice swings. When you practice swing, note where the club head brushes the ground. When you get ready to hit the ball on this shot, place your feet in relation to the ball, where the club head brushed the ground. If you have an uphill or downhill stance, the ball location at address will be forward or backward of your usual setup. With severe downhill lies, I sometimes play the ball uphill of (outside of) my back foot.

If you do this, remember to adjust your aim and your timing so that you are hitting the ball on the anticipated line, and not way to the right.

This must be a smooth stroke, not jerky. Watch the pros on TV. And here's the real secret of the chip shot. **The club head stays very close to the ground on the backswing, just like putting.** The chip shot is only an extension of the putt, and just like the putt, you must keep the club head low to the ground.

Again I tell you, watch the pros hit this shot. Notice that they do not lift the club on the backswing unless they are trying to hit the ball into the air, over a hazard.

Another important point. Don't rush this shot. It is a comfortable, relaxed shot. Just start your backswing, gather yourself at the peak of the backswing, and swing a controlled, smooth swing <u>accelerating</u> through the ball. It is easier using only the shoulders, rather than the small, jerky wrist and arm muscles. And certainly, control your body. There should be no swaying motion and no movement of the head during this swing, only the shoulders rotating in the magic move.

(When I say "gather yourself" at the top of the backswing, I mean: slow down, even stop momentarily. One reason most golfers have trouble with this and with other strokes, is because they are moving their arms forward, while their shoulders are still going backward. Stop everything going backward. Then **smoothly**, start everything going forward together.)

Fifteen minutes in your back yard will do wonders for this shot, giving you confidence in it, in how to play it, and giving you a feel for how hard to hit it. When you get a chance, show up at the course early, before teeing off, drop a few balls beside the chipping or putting green and practice this shot. **You'll see immediate improvement in your scores.**

Another tip. If you have a short (especially downhill) chip, don't chip it, putt it. One of the first lessons to learn, is that the putter is not exclusively for the green. Often a difficult chip can be hit closer to the hole by using the putter. Think. Use your judgment. And, if sometime, you hit a really bad short chip, remember that the next time, and try putting the ball.

Another good idea about chipping: Be conscious of the length of your backswing and your follow through. Actually look at the club head during a practice swing. Make a few practice swings of how far you want to swing back, and how far you want to follow through, then, when hitting the actual shot, use that practice to guide your swing. Remember, your brain is a computer...input, process, output. Put the information into your computer, then, when you need it, retrieve it.

The best practice for chipping is to go to the putting or chipping green, and just hit a bunch of chips at a particular hole. Try to hit the ball close or into the hole, easily, without strain or pressure. It's an easy shot, and you'll get the hang of it.

Or put a towel on the green 15 or 20 feet away, then try to land the ball on the towel. Or get a bushel basket and try to hit balls into it from 15 feet away.

When I was a better golfer, I used to go to the chipping green and hit 150 chips for practice at least once a week. I expected to sink one chip in 11, and to put the rest within one putt distance.

If you do nothing but improve your putting, chipping, and how to think on the course, you'll break 90.

CHAPTER 5: PITCHING

The pitch shot is just an extension of the chip shot, only from 20-50 yards from the green.

Again, keep the head and spine still. Again, rotate the shoulders with the magic move. Again, back elbow in against your body, **short backswing**, gather yourself and **accelerate** through the ball with an appropriate follow-through.

Depending on how far you are from the green, you'll probably need to co-ordinate a little weight transfer with this shot...weight back with the backswing, and forward on the throughswing.

And, you'll need to introduce some wrist action. Remember, the wrists should swing like a gate, and the gate must be square to the line of flight (close the gate) at impact of the club head with the ball. (Or paddle the child.)

This is a finesse shot, not a power shot. This is not a full swing. Unlike with the driver, you are not trying to hit the ball for distance. You know the exact distance you want the ball to go so it will end up at the hole. There is no question of whether you can reach that distance with the club in your hand.

Control that distance as well as you can. If you practice in your back yard, you will have a feel for how far the ball goes, and how hard to hit it. And be aware, it does not have to fly to the green. Hit it hard enough to get to your target. It isn't important whether it flys, bounces along, or rolls.

This is a very important shot. Hit it well, and you have a tap-in for a par. Hit it badly, and you may wind up with a double bogey or worse. These are the shots that control your score more than your drives and long irons. Badly missed long shots can be overcome with good, accurate short shots; good pitching, chipping, and putting.

And this shot can be practiced in your back yard, the same as the chip shot. Make or pick a target 30 or 40 or 50 yards away, (a rag or a towel or one of your children's toys left out in the yard) and hit balls to it. A fun game is to make a backyard golf course, and hit different distances from toy to toy.

By the way, it's a good idea to save your old, used up balls, and keep them for practice. If you lose balls on the course, and don't have many used ones to keep, look in any golf magazine, and you'll find used balls for sale for about $3 a dozen. You can buy a bag for practice balls, or just use an old gym bag or laundry bag.

After reading this book helps you improve your game, you'll have a lot of left-over balls, because you'll stop losing them. I personally, buy about a dozen new balls to last a year, and at the end of the year, with a few found balls, I usually have some left over…and I play about 100 rounds of golf a year.

***

Let's talk about the "flop shot". Which shot do you think would be easier for distance control? A low, short shot, or a high short shot? How hard do you hit a high short shot to make it go high, but only a short distance? And what if you don't catch it just right? How far might it go?

I believe that it's smart to be gentle with this shot. Only hit the ball high enough off the ground to keep it on line. All you want with this shot is to put it somewhere on the green, so you can get down in two putts and walk away with your 5.

Blasting these shots is not the answer. Control is the answer.

So, I recommend a narrow stance, a short backswing, magic move, and accelerate through the ball only hard enough to get the ball to the hole. Then follow through straight down the line toward the target, to promote accuracy.

(A way to measure backswing: Think of your backswing along the circle, inserting the face of a clock into the circle. A backswing with your arms pointing straight back, parallel to the ground is at 3 o'clock. Only going back half that far, would be 4 or 5 o'clock, etc. With your practice swing, set the time at 3 or 4 o'clock, and accelerate through the shot. Then duplicate that "time" on the actual hit.)

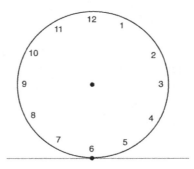

CAPTION: The swing circle with the face of a clock inserted.

Before each round, it is smart to loosen up with a bucket of balls on the practice range. Get the stiffness out of your muscles. Get your timing right. Prepare yourself for the game. Put new input into your "computer brain". Again, watch the pros. They show up an hour before their tee time, hit balls, practice chipping and putting. They are ready to start scoring on the first hole with their first swing.

Without the proper warm-up, it takes 3-5 holes to get yourself grooved. But the last thing I do, before leaving the driving range, is to pick a target, 30 or 40 yards away, and hit the last half dozen balls to it, just to get the feel for that distance.

Then when I'm on the course, my computer brain, having recently stored the memories of the practice chips, outputs the information of how hard to hit that 40 yard pitch on the course to put it on the green.

Placement of the ball for this shot should be about in the middle of your stance. Just like with the chip shot practice, take a practice swing and see where your club head brushes the grass, then place the ball there in relation to your feet.

***

This might be a good time to discuss a bit of basic strategy. Often, a golfer will find himself near the green, but with some kind of hazard between himself and the flagstick, usually a sand trap or a grass bunker, or water, or just uneven ground.

If the pitch shot is not hit well, is chili-dipped, topped, or just hit too softly, the ball ends up in the hazard. There are two schools of thought regarding this situation.

The first school says that, no matter what, don't leave the ball in the hazard. Hit it hard, and get it past the trap. But, there may be another hazard of some kind beyond the hole, and a ball hit too hard, or bladed might go there. Besides, this strategy puts additional pressure on the golfer, increasing the chance of a bad shot.

The second school remembers that the goal is to land the ball **on the green**, and two putt. So the better chance is to aim for the green, and **not for the hole.** See if there isn't a direction to go where the hazard is avoided altogether. Almost always there is a route to the green around the hazard, a route that could even allow the ball to be rolled onto the green. Taking that direction, hitting the pitch becomes almost automatic. This will remove most of the pressure from the golfer, and increase the chance to hit a good shot, or, conversely, to get away with a bad shot.

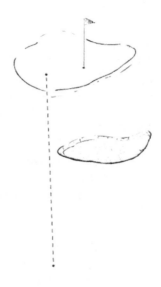

CAPTION: Aim for the green, not the hole, and avoid the bunker.

Remember, the goal with pitching, is to put the ball **somewhere on the green**, then two putt. Once you've had a chance to practice this shot, you will expect to put the ball close to the hole for occasional one-putts. **But to start, just get it somewhere on the green.**

***

Here's another important tip. Sometimes, you have a short 8 or 9 iron distance to the green, but there's a tree or other impediment over your line of flight, which, if you hit the short iron, will catch the ball flying too high.

There is no rule that you must use the 8 or 9 iron. Take a longer, lower lofted club, a 4 or 5 iron, and hit the ball under the obstacle. If you choke down on the club, and take less than a full swing (always remembering to still accelerate) the ball will go the shorter distance, and with the softer stroke, will fly even lower.

***

Now for one of my pet peeves in golf: the "too long" backswing on short shots. I never understand why any golfer will take the same backswing on a 30 yard pitch shot as he takes when hitting his driver. Just reading that sentence should indicate to you what a really stupid thing that is.

With a driver, you are trying to hit the ball as far as you can. With every other shot in the bag, there should be no question of if you can hit the ball far enough. You are holding your 100 yard club to hit a 100 yard shot; or your 150 yard club for a 150 yard shot. You know you can hit the ball that far with that club. **The goal is no longer distance, it is accuracy**! Hitting the ball onto the green, close to the hole! And for greater accuracy, you should hit with control. For control, shorten that backswing, and accelerate through the ball.

And for half-shots, from 50 or 30 or 20 yards, short backswing, accelerate, and follow through.

There is no need to extend your backswing to driver length when you are no longer trying to power the ball as far as you can. It is almost impossible to take a long backswing, then try to hit a short shot without decelerating into the ball. **Deceleration is the biggest single reason for chili-dipped pitches and chips.**

Talking about control, reminds me of an experience watching Sam Snead. I was raised in West Virginia, as was Snead. In 1958, the W.Va. State Open was played at Lakeview Country Club in Morgantown, my home course, and Sam played, and won. I was at the practice tee when Sam emptied his bag of practice balls and told his caddy to pick up his ball bag, and to go out about 150 yards on the range, and he'd hit balls to him.

The kid said, "You want me to go out on the range so you can hit balls at me?"

And Sam said, "I said I'll hit balls <u>to</u> you, not <u>at</u> you."

After some convincing, the caddy went out, and Sam started hitting 7 irons to him. The kid stood there, one hand holding the ball bag, and Snead hit balls his caddy could catch on one bounce.

The caddy just stood there. He didn't have to move. The balls bounced in front of him, he stuck his hand out, and they bounced into his hand, and he caught them and put them into the ball bag.

All this time, Mike, our pro was describing the course to Sam, who had never played Lakeview, nor even seen it.

When you can do what Sam Snead could do, then you can expect to break par. But if you can't regularly hit a 10,000 square foot green with a 7 iron, don't even think about breaking par. Just try to play bogey golf!

Sam got that good by hitting millions of balls in practice.

You can't expect to practice like Sam Snead, but you can spend 15 minutes, one evening a month in your back yard, getting the feel of those very important pitch shots and chip shots, which will cut 5 to 10 shots a round off your scores.

CHAPTER 6: HOW TO HIT THE BALL, STRAIGHT

The full golf swing is just an extension of the pitch shot, but with power.

And the power can come from rhythm and timing, not necessarily "killing" the ball.

I have a cousin, Mike, who's about 15 years younger than I. One day, in Phoenix, my father, my father-in-law, and I, took Mike, who was about 12 (and looked like he was 8) out to play golf with us. We came to a short par 4, and we three adults tried to reach the green off the tee by swinging harder. We all missed our shots.

Mike, knowing he couldn't reach the green, hit his usual rhythmic shot, and outdrove the three of us.

As we walked down the fairway, I said to Mike, "You see, it's not how hard you swing, it's the timing and the rhythm in your swing. Do you use the Rhythm Method Mike?"

"Aw" Fred," he said, "I don't know what the Rhythm Method is."

I told that story at Mike's wedding reception. Mike is now a doctor, and knows all about the Rhythm

Method. His response was, "All these years, I looked up to you like a big brother, now I find out you were only making fun of me." We both laughed. But Lil, Mike's wife, has not forgiven me!

***

I must confess, it is hard for me to understand how a person can enjoy golf, shooting 120 and worse, missing, slicing, and pull-hooking shots into the woods. To me, that's no fun.

Most of the people I play with are impressed with my game. They all out-hit me for distance. Many of them, now that I'm getting older and sicker and weaker, are outscoring me. Rarely does anybody ever comment on their length or their score. But every time I play with strangers, they comment on how straight I hit the ball. "Doesn't it get boring always hitting from the fairway?" they ask.

"Boring is good." is my standard reply.

I think hitting the ball for a long distance is the most overrated factor in golf. Once when I was younger, I tested my theory. I took all the clubs longer than a 5 iron out of my bag and played 9 holes. I shot 43. Playing that for 18 would be 86, easily breaking 90.

I once knew a youngster who couldn't hit the ball farther than 150-160 yards, and he carried a 3 handicap.

In olden times, when I lived in West Virginia, and Sam Snead was still at the Greenbrier, I went there sometimes for a week-end. On the bulletin board in the pro shop, they had some of Sam's score cards. One was the best score Sam had on the Old White Course with **nothing but a 7 iron**...no driver, no putter, no sand wedge, just a 7 iron. The score was 70. Is distance overrated?

Gary Player, who has won 164 golf tournaments all around the world, is not a long hitter. He never was. In the 1960's when he was winning the Masters, the US Open (at Bellerive, at 7450 yards, the longest course in Open history to that time), the British Open, and the PGA, his average driving distance was less than 255 yards.

Once, at an exhibition at a course he didn't know in Yakima, WA, he asked his caddy to club him. The caddy, who was the state amateur champion, said, "From here, I usually use a 6 iron, but you're so short, you'd better use a 5."

Or Calvin Peete, the most famous for being a short hitter. Calvin only hit the ball 245 yards off the tee. But he won the Vardon Trophy (twice), for the lowest scoring average on Tour, and finished in the top 4 on the Tour Money List 3 times in his 12 year career. But, over his career, he hit an amazing 80% of all fairways off the tee!

Or Lee Trevino, Tom Kite, Lanny Wadkins, names on an endless list of short hitting professional major tournament winners.

Distance is nice. It isn't crucial. Control is crucial. Knowing how to hit the shot you want, then hitting it.

That's how to score on a golf course. Knowing which shot even to try, is crucial. Knowing what you can do, and what you can't do, and what will be easy and automatic, or what is nearly impossible at your skill level, and then, playing the automatic good shot is crucial.

Just because you've seen a professional hit a ball over a 50 foot tree that's 25 yards in front of him over a pond, onto a green 160 yards away, doesn't mean that shot is in **your** bag! He hits 500 balls a day. You don't. He practices that shot hour after hour. You don't. He gets paid to make that shot. You don't.

Whatever your profession is. Whatever you do for a living. Do you imagine any professional golfer could do it as well as you do it on Monday? You probably can't do his job as well as he can do it on Saturday.

Pappy said, "Never bet against a man at **his** game."

Remembering this, let's start improving **your** golf game, and increase your pleasure by improving your aptitude and decreasing your scores.

***

It is important to know how far you hit each club with a smooth, controlled swing. Starting with your wedges, and progressing back to your driver, you should find a place, usually a driving range, pick a target, at a known distance, and try to hit it. Or, with one of these new GPS distance finders, you can measure your shots on the course.

Generally, depending on how strong you are, how coordinated your swing, and how far you normally hit the ball, your clubs are designed for them to progress 5 to 15 yards from club to club.

For example, in the 1970's and 80's, before club and ball design improved to their 21st century efficiency, and when I was young and strong, I hit:

Driver.....................225-230 yards
3 wood......................210 yards
4 wood......................200 yards
5 wood......................185 yards
3 iron........................170 yards
4 iron........................160 yards
5 iron........................150 yards
6 iron........................140 yards
7 iron.........................135 yards
8 iron.........................120 yards
9 iron.........................105 yards
sand wedge...................65 yards
Those were the 12 clubs I carried, plus a putter, of course.

Here's my point. If I had 150 yards to the green, I hit my 5 iron, unless there was some good reason not to. I knew that with an easy, controlled swing, I would hit the 5 iron 150 yards...straight.

***

Before you start hitting the ball, let's talk about Pre-Shot Routine.

Your teaching pro will probably omit this from your lessons, but **pre Shot Routine is critically important** to hitting the ball, hitting it well, and hitting it straight.

One thing almost every golfer who can't break 90 does, is overlook this very important part of the golf swing, and the few who have a pre-shot routine usually do it badly.

Here are some examples of **bad** pre-shot routines.

1. <u>Hitting the ball without aiming at your target</u>. Virtually every golf course I have ever played, had some tee boxes which were aimed at trouble...woods, water, etc. Most high handicappers just tee up the ball, then hit in whatever direction the tee suggests... right into the trouble. And they don't aim at a target on other shots, either.

2. <u>Taking too many practice swings</u>. Some golfers swing 4 or 5 or more practice swings before each shot. If they score 120, they have swung the club 500 times in a round of golf. I'll bet they're pretty tired late in the round, and I'll bet their scores late in the round show it.

3. <u>Aiming at a target, then moving your feet</u>. Once you are set up to hit at your target, **do not move your feet**! That changes your aim! I have seen high handicappers line up their shot, then back away, take a practice swing, then step back to their ball, and not check their alignment again. Or, they waggle, move their feet, waggle, move their feet, etc.

Let me tell you something. If you are aimed in the wrong direction, your computer-brain knows it, and will tell you, "Don't hit this shot." "DON'T HIT THIS SHOT." **"MY GOD! DON'T HIT THIS SHOT!!!"**

Then, if you insist on hitting it, still aiming in the wrong direction, your brain will interfere, trying to adjust to the misalignment, and you will almost certainly miss the shot. This scenario is the cause of about ½ of your missed shots. Your brain is trying to keep you from hitting a ball into the woods!

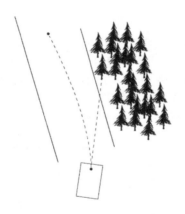

CAPTION: This picture shows the tee box aimed at trouble, not at the fairway. Be careful. There are a lot of tees lined up like this.

4. <u>Taking the **wrong** practice swing</u>. Having an uphill lie, and taking a practice swing in some other direction than the uphill shot. In other words, putting the wrong information into their computer brain immediately prior to hitting the shot.

This is a correct Pre-Shot Routine.

• Decide which club to hit.

• If you wish, take a practice swing, practicing the shot you are about to hit…level if your lie is level; uphill if your lie is uphill; ball above your feet if the ball is above your feet, etc.

• Stand behind your ball and pick a target. Then sight a line from your target back to your ball, and pick a spot that you want your ball to go over about 12 inches in front of your ball, like a bowler picks a spot to roll his ball over.

• Take your stance, setting up so that your club face is aimed over your spot, and once you are set, **do not move your feet.**

• Waggle your club. Check your aim. Waggle your club. Check your aim. Hit the ball.

If you ever see Jack Nicklaus hit a ball on TV, watch his eyes when he addresses his ball. He is aiming over his spot! (But, in his case, it looks like he is using 2 spots, which is a bit much for us duffers.)

Golf is a game of constancy; and constancy is gained by knowing your routine, and by repeating your routine over and over. Every good golfer knows that he must repeat his same routine before every shot. **If he is interrupted by a distraction of some kind, He will begin his routine again.**

***

This chapter is How to Hit the Ball…Straight. First, how to hit the ball at all, then, straight.

There are 3 parts to the golf swing: 1.. The Address. 2. The Backswing. and 3. The Through-swing and Follow-through.

(We have already discussed the grip extensively. The most important things to remember about the grip are that you must hold the club in a way that lets your brain and your muscles execute properly. And you must be conscious of the club, its location and its attitude. The grip does all this if you grip in the sensitive parts of the hand...the fingers, and if you align the club properly, putting the face of the club on the same plane as the palms of your hands.)

1. The address is easy, because you can slowly and deliberately take your place. Take your stance exactly where you want it, and as you want it. And see that everything is perfect before you start your swing. If you notice, the pros are very careful about how they set themselves up to the ball before every swing... drive to putt.

Essentially, here is what you must do:
- Take a good grip on the club.
- Go through your pre-shot routine.
- Set your feet a comfortable distance apart, square to the target. (Square to the target means that a line extending from your back toe, past your front toe, will extend straight to the target.) Most pros begin with the feet approximately shoulder distance apart. Many golfers keep that as their preferred position, but many spread them farther apart, or bring them closer together. It really isn't

important, whatever is most comfortable for you.

- Set your feet so that the ball is a little bit closer to your front foot than to your back foot. If you are right handed, the ball should be about in front of your heart, not your breast bone.
- Flex your knees, a little, and pull the rear one inward, under your body.
- Bend over from the waist, keeping your butt well back
- Place the club head immediately behind the ball, extending your left elbow out, away from your body, and pulling your **right elbow in against your body** (again, for right handed golfers). This elbow arrangement has the effect of lifting your left shoulder, and thrusting it forward toward the ball, and lowering your right shoulder, and pulling it back away from the ball. **With your elbows thus set, your shoulders will be aimed to the right of your target, thus in an inside-out attitude, thus promoting an inside to outside swing.**
- Lift your chin. When you make the magic move, your front shoulder will come back around in front of you. You want the shoulder to move UNDER your chin, and not bump into your chin (and move your head).
- It is usually assumed that your weight at address will be about equally distributed between your toes and your heels, and equally distributed on both feet.
- The clubhead should be placed behind the ball, with the ball centered, but a little bit

closer to the toe of the club face. Your swing will cause some centrifugal force, and pull the club head a little bit farther away from you.

All of the above can be accomplished slowly, simply, and deliberately, with a minimum of error.

CAPTION: Keep your chin up so your shoulder can pass under it.

2. The back swing is the last thing you do to put yourself in position to hit the ball well. Again it can be accomplished slowly and deliberately. There is no need to rush. You can put yourself into a perfect posi-

tion, so that, with some practice, you can hit the ball well and straight. A fast backswing will not help you hit the ball farther. You are not moving the ball with your backswing.

- <u>Always keeping your head and spine in the same location</u>, your right elbow in against your body, and your left arm reasonably straight, turn back with the magic move, initiating it with your shoulders. Do not move your head up or down, right or left. Your shoulders will turn your hips away from your target. (Remember, the magic move is **rotating your shoulders around your spine**. It should feel like swinging inside a big barrel.) At the same time, transfer your weight to the **inside** of your back foot, keeping your **back knee flexed**. And keeping your **butt back**! At the top of your backswing, your **back** should be almost facing your target.
- Cock your right wrist back, so that at the top of your backswing, your right hand and arm feel that they are **in the position of a waiter carrying a tray**. (This is very important. Remember how, earlier, I had your hands "praying", and I said the proper wrist action is like swinging a gate? Well, at the top of your backswing, the gate is fully open, and your elbow is directly under it, like a waiter...)
- Always remember the circle of the swing described earlier. Keeping your head and spine in the same place, take the club head back away from the ball with your shoulders, and let your shoulders move your arms

back, **low and slow in one solid_movement**. Feel the ground with the bottom of the club for about a foot backing away from the ball, and let the club head naturally rise up smoothly above and behind your shoulders, bringing it back to the inside. Don't try to raise it too high, let the magic move place it comfortably back there. Don't take it back too far. You'll lose balance and control and make hitting the ball tougher than it has to be. A short backswing will help you connect with the ball better, centering your hit on the sweet spot and actually giving you more power.

- Finally, it is important that you start from a balanced position at address, and maintain good balance all the way back to the top of your backswing. The secret of balance is keeping your head still and keeping your butt back.

Are you ready? As you are about to hit the ball, remember that you want this to be a controlled swing. How many times, after missing the shot, has a golfer in your hearing said, "Damn! I tried to kill it!"?

CAPTION: Waiter carrying a tray, with his hand and arm in perfect position for the top of the backswing.

***

As I have told you above, all your clubs should be rated by you...how far you can hit them with a controlled, smooth swing. The important thing is that your 125 yard club goes 125 yards. Because you need 125 yards, use the right club with a smooth, easy swing, hit it well, and get the 125 yards you need. It doesn't matter what some other player uses for 125 yards. Use what is comfortable for you. You've heard the term, "Playing within yourself". That's what it means.

A few pros hit their average drive 320 yards. Most don't. Some, playing within themselves, hit it only 280, giving away 40 yards per drive. Yet, a lot of those 280 yard drivers win tournaments. It isn't a game of how far **can** you hit the ball. It's how far **will** you hit the ball!

3. The <u>throughswing</u> is the only part of the swing that can not be slowly controlled and manipulated.

Essentially, it begins with the "gathering" or pause at the top of the backswing, where **everything** stops... and restarts, **smoothly** moving in the opposite direction **together**.

At this point, you must be smooth and controlled. Again watch the pros. They are all positively "oily" as Sam Snead used to say. There is only one good pro who "jumps" at the ball from the top of his backswing, unfortunately for you and me, its Tiger Woods. He must know something, that apparently, nobody else does.

I have to break in here with a comment. Almost every pro I've ever talked to says that the power in the golf swing is generated by the front arm (left arm for righties) pulling the club through the swing. I have to say that, I've always thought of the golf swing as being right armed. The feeling I get is of throwing a ball in a side-armed motion, or hitting a low tennis forehand shot. (Or paddling a fraternity brother.)

I believe that, if you look closely at Ben Hogan's swing, you'll see that he drives the swing with his right arm. You can see it especially in his follow-thru. Watch it next time you get the chance...he's hitting with his right arm!

And I further believe that, trying to power the swing with an **unnatural** pulling motion creates a centrifugal force that causes delayed hand action, and an outside-to-inside club head path, which exaggerates all those big slices.

And finally, by thinking of the golf swing as being right armed, much of the "mystique" is removed from the swing, and the golfer reacts naturally just as if he were throwing a ball sidearm, or was hitting a tennis forehand shot. Actually, the golf swing is that natural.

***

Now, getting back to the swing, gather yourself at the top, and begin your swing by transferring your weight to your left (front) toe, while you unwind the magic move at your shoulders, and **keep your right (back) elbow in against your body.** Increase your shoulder and arm and hand speed (accelerate) into, and past the ball. But, as your hands reach a point, approximately outside your right (back) thigh, begin to uncock your wrists, **_so that your palms and the face of your club will be perpendicular to the line of flight and pointing at your target at the moment of contact with the ball._**

As the clubhead passes through the position where the ball was sitting, waiting to be hit, **continue accelerating**, and straighten both elbows. The path of the club head should go down the line of flight, and then up and over your left shoulder, finally stopping around behind your head.

In an ideal swing, your head and spine stay in the same position until after the ball is hit. Moving your head forward as you swing not only moves the club head circle, it actually slows the club head. So, keep your head back until after the ball is away.

And those are the 3 parts of the swing...simple... right?

There are some unique thoughts on the swing that you've probably not heard before; some questions about the importance of this or that. Let me explain.

First of all, how close or how far from the ball should you be at address. That's a matter of comfort for the individual golfer, mostly based on height. The shorter you are, the farther you are from your ball, the flatter your swing will be, and the easier it will be to make the magic move. But, remember, if you get too far away, balance becomes a problem, and the flatter your swing, the lower the flight of your ball and the more likely you are to top it.

On the other hand, you taller golfers, standing closer to the ball promotes an upright swing, which makes the magic move more difficult (you start swaying and "lifting" the shoulders, instead of turning). But your ball flight will be higher.

Anywhere between too close and too far should be acceptable. Whatever is comfortable for you. I have a pretty flat swing, and, and although it works for me, I have difficulty putting backspin on the ball, and stopping it when hitting over obstacles close to the green. But when your longest drive is only 180 yards, you really aren't interested in backing the ball up!

Jack Nicklaus had a very upright swing. And since he was the greatest golfer in the world, everybody started copying his upright swing, and we got a lot of weird golf swings. Ben Hogan, on the other hand, was pretty emphatic about keeping the swing "circle" on a plane determined by the distance the golfer stood from the ball, the farther away, the flatter the swing.

Secondly, keeping your butt back is a swing key not many think about. But try this: Assume an address position, butt back, of course. Then, slowly try to swing at the ball, giving yourself a little "extra" body push with your hips. You see what happens...as your butt comes forward, it levers your head up. Your head comes up, the swing circle comes up, and you'll top the ball.

So, keep your butt back. Make the magic move with your **shoulders** and keep your head and spine constant.

Initiating your swing by transferring your weight to your left (front) toe is important for several reasons.

Firstly, it gives you the extra power of the weight shift. Secondly, it helps you keep your head in the same (down) position and your butt back. And thirdly, it moves your momentum into the ball. (Remember, the ball is forward in your stance...if you don't shift your weight forward, you'll hit behind the ball.)

How about taking a divot? Most good golfers do take a divot after hitting the ball. They swing down on the ball "pinching" it with the ground, to put backspin on it which lifts it into the air for a longer, higher flight pattern.

But some great golfers, like Tom Watson (and me) are sweepers. I grew up with an aversion to damaging the golf course, so I always tried to hit the ball cleanly, without taking a divot, and learned too late that I should be taking one. By that time, my swing was grooved, and I've just always been a sweeper.

By the way, I'm a TERRIBLE ball striker. I only score well because I think well on the course, know my capabilities (or lack of them) and don't try anything beyond my ability to execute.

Bending the knees inward is important because, the back knee, bent inward acts as a brake, keeping you from moving your head back and up during the backswing. It keeps the head still, and promotes better contact with the ball.

***

The next two items, the right elbow, and the wrist action are factors in hitting the ball straight...also the shoulder setup at address.

There are two factors in causing a slice, a hook, or a straight shot right down the middle of the fairway: (1) the direction the club head is moving as it strikes the ball; and (2) the angle of the club face as it hits the ball.

The path of the club head can be inside-out, or outside-in, or straight toward the target. The ideal is straight toward the target. Worst is cutting across the ball, outside-in, which is how the overwhelming majority of golfers hit the ball, which is why they are slicers. The club head cuts across the ball outside to inside, with the delayed wrist action that all the pros teach, putting maximum left to right English on the ball, thus causing the slice.

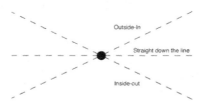

CAPTION The three possible paths of the clubhead.

Most golfers cut across the ball, outside to inside because they are positioned to do that at address. Here's why.

Your left hand on the grip of the club is closer to your body than your right hand. The natural set of the shoulders resulting from this hand position is right shoulder forward, left shoulder back, causing an outside to inside shoulder plane (aiming left of the target), and the swing, naturally and automatically, follows the shoulders.

You cure this, in the address position I've described, with the left elbow straight, and out, away from the body, and the right elbow bent and in against the body, this causes the plane of the shoulders to be inside to outside, aimed to the right of the target. And the swing will naturally and automatically follow the plane of the shoulders, inside to outside, or straight down the line toward the target.

Watch a pro on TV swing. Notice his right upper arm throughout the swing. With most of them, Tiger included, that right upper arm is always close to his body. If it ever gets very far away from his body, his right hand rises away from the swing path, causing a "casting" of the club, and that's when lots of bad things start to happen.

Even Jack Nicklaus, with his famous flying elbow, always got that right arm back to his body before hitting the ball...or else he hit a bad shot.

Keep that right upper arm against your body until after the moment of impact with the ball, then, straighten your elbows and begin your follow-through.

I can't overemphasize the position of the right elbow. In fact, it is a very important secret of the golf swing, from short putts to long drives. **On all shots**, that right elbow should stay against your body until after the ball is hit. This position makes the magic move so easy as to be almost automatic. It helps to influence your swing in the matter of keeping your head in the same place. It influences the proper shoulder turn on the backswing, it maintains the inside to outside attitude of the through swing.

Also, keeping the right elbow in against the body coordinates the body and arm movement, tying them together, so that your arms and your body work together. Both are attacking the ball from the same direction at the same time. Again, watch the pros on TV. Their arms and bodies work in harmony, together, not separately.

Now, about the wrist action. Just about every pro I've ever heard about teaches delayed wrist action. Big Mistake!!! (The worst slices are caused by cutting across the ball with your clubface open because you delayed your wrist action too long!) It's OK for the pros who, hitting thousands of practice balls are perfecting their timing and wrist action by working on it day after day on the driving range (and building the strength of their wrists). But we amateurs don't have all that much time to perfect the golf swing, and many of us have weak wrists. We need a short cut. And this is it. Go to a driving range, and with one bucket of balls, you can learn to hit the ball straight.

First, practice by swinging your club level, like a baseball bat. Keep your right elbow in all throughout the backswing and back to the ball. You want the club face to be square at impact, so the wrist uncocking must begin earlier than you've been doing it. Close the gate! Translate that to the golf swing, and you'll see it should begin when your hands are somewhere along about the outside of the right thigh as you are swinging into the ball.

(Remember what I told you when describing the grip. If your hands are on the same plane as the club face, you always know which way the club is aimed... the same as the palm of your back hand!)

Next, with a 5, 6, or 7 iron, address a ball, with the correct shoulder plane (inside-out), left arm straight, right arm bent, in against the body. And here's the key. At the top of the backswing, that right elbow must still be in against your body and your wrists cocked (waiter carrying a tray).

Start with slow-motion, little waist-high half-swings, slowly trying to get the feel for the inside-outside swing, and trying to perfect your timing by transferring your weight and swinging that "wrist-gate, so that the_*plane of your hands (and the plane of the club face) at impact with the ball is_perpendicular to the line of flight.* Pick a specific target close by, maybe 100 yards or so away, and aim for it.

Hit a few balls with that half swing. Watch them go straight toward your target. (And notice how far they go without your having to kill the ball. But remember… accelerate! and follow through!) Then, gradually, as you become comfortable with the new feel, increase your speed and rhythm to full swing and speed.

But be careful with this wrist timing. Closing the gate too soon is equally wrong, and will cause you to hit fat, behind the ball.

That's the secret. Palms same plane as the club face, plane of the shoulders inside-out…right elbow in against your body, left elbow out away from your body setting up that plane…magic move…waiter carrying a tray at the top of the back swing…right upper arm attached to the body until impact…and (close the gate) **wrist action squaring the club face at impact**.

Try this at half speed until it feels natural and until you get the timing right. Coordinate your body with your hands, so that shoulders, hips, hands and wrists are all square (perpendicular to the flight of the ball) at impact. **Remember, you are inputting this information to your computer-brain for later access.**

If you do what I say, I guarantee that, with one bucket of balls at the driving range, your slice will be gone, and you'll see that, with a little adjustment, <u>you will be able to hit fades, draws, and straight balls on demand by adjusting your shoulder plane and the timing of your wrists at impact.</u>

And here's another tip. Try to use a relatively short backswing and swing slower than usual, but **always accelerating through the ball.** With the shorter backswing and keeping your right elbow against your body, it's more likely you'll hit the ball flush. And hitting the ball flush with good timing, makes the ball go farther.

Also, you're less likely to move your head on your backswing. Believe it or not, more bad shots are caused by golfers **_moving their heads on the backswing_** than most people realize.

"You peeked". Doesn't always mean your head came up as you were swinging through the ball. Almost as often, it means, "You moved your head (up, or down, or back) _during the backswing_."

Lastly, remember that hitting for long distance: drives, fairway woods, hybrids and long irons, is not important as long as you can hit the ball a reasonable distance, and keep it in play. It is good to remember that tip I gave you about chipping and pitching... "gather" yourself at the top of your backswing. Pause.

Stop everything going backward. Then, **smoothly**, start everything going forward, together. With control. Accelerating into the ball and through the ball.

The secret to breaking 90, or 80, or 70, is three rules:
Rule 1. Keep the ball in play. (Don't go into the woods, or the water, or out of bounds.)
And Rules 2 & 3. Chip and Putt like a genius.

I have never been a good ball striker. But in my youth, I was a 6 handicap, who almost always scored between 78 and 82. My home course, Columbia (SC) Country Club stretched to over 7200 yards off the back tees, and I often played the back tees. My game was: short and straight, don't do anything foolish, and stay away from trouble, and master the easy shots (chips, pitches, and putts).

Tiger Woods is the greatest golfer who ever lived. Whether he ever beats Jack Nicklaus' records or not, he's already done things Jack never did, like win 7 Tour tournaments in a row or hold all 4 major trophies at the same time.

But Tiger's game is not the best off the tee. He is neither the longest nor the straightest driver. His game is not even the best with long second shots, although his long game is terrific. Tiger's secret is that, from 150 yards in, he can put the ball closer to the hole more often than any other golfer who has ever lived. And besides that, as if he needed more, he is the best putter who ever lived...especially with long putts.

Tiger Woods exemplifies Rules 2 & 3, chipping and putting like a genius, better than any golfer who ever lived. That's why he's the best ever.

Now that you know how to hit the ball, and why things work as they do, you need to know one more thing.

Every great golfer, from Hagen to Hogan to Nicklaus to Woods had his own swing. None of them were (or are) perfect, classic swings. They all swung the club their own way. And now, you have to personalize your swing to work for you. There are going to be individual parts of the classic swing that don't work for you...like maybe, you hit better with an open or closed stance, rather than square. Or setting up with the ball forward or farther back than in front of your heart. Or you feel more comfortable choking down on your grip.

You'll have to discover yourself what works for you, and what doesn't. But, at least you know what basic moves are important, what can and cannot be changed, and, most important, <u>why</u> you do what you do.

CHAPTER 7: SAND SHOTS, UNEVEN LIES, AND OTHER TOUGH SHOTS.

Every pro and every player has a solution to hitting these difficult shots. Before you go out on the course, see if you can't find a driving range that has sidehill, uphill, downhill and sand areas for practice. Try to get some experience hitting these shots before you try them on the course. They are not impossible to hit well. But they should be practiced to give you an indication of what you, personally can expect when these situations arise.

AND REMEMBER!!! THERE IS A SPECIAL PLACE IN HELL FOR THOSE WHO DO NOT RAKE SAND TRAPS... CAREFULLY AND WELL!!! AND YOU SHOULD LEAVE THE RAKE "IN" THE TRAP WITH THE HANDLE A LITTLE OUTSIDE THE TRAP!!

GREENSIDE SAND SHOTS: I've already told you, greenside sand shots are the easiest shots in golf...you don't even have to hit the ball.

I used to play golf with a pretty girl when I was in college. She told me her way to hit sand shots. She just put her chin on her chest and hit her usual shot. It worked every time for her, but it never worked for me. I guess she just had a better chest.

But this is another shot that's easy to perfect with a little bit of knowledge and a little bit of practice.

First, you **must** have a sand wedge. (If you don't own one, it is important that you get one.)

Pick up your sand wedge so that the toe of the club head is facing you, and the club shaft is pointing away from you. Notice that under the leading edge of the club there is an over-sized bulge of metal. That bulge is called the "bounce". And it's there for a purpose.

What the good sand player knows is that the face of the sand wedge is not the face of the sand wedge. The face of the sand wedge is the leading edge of the bounce.

Let me explain. When you try to hit out of a sand trap the part of the club that moves the ball is not the face. Unlike all your other clubs, it is the bounce of the sand wedge that does the work, by moving the sand; and the sand moves the ball.

Go to a sand trap (Hopefully your course has a practice trap.) Drop a few balls on smooth sand and take a good stance, digging your feet down to a solid footing. Now, thinking of the bounce as the face of the club, lay the real clubface flat, facing skyward, then, using the bounce as the face of the club, hit a spot in the sand about one inch behind the ball. Continue under the ball until you've taken a fairly flat divot about the size of a dollar bill, then continue your swing through your follow through.

If you've done this, the ball has come out of the trap very easily, and you've learned one of the advantages of being a short hitter. The ball doesn't go very far. You don't have to worry about hitting it too far.

This shot is really easy. Easy to get out of the trap, and easy to feel how hard to hit the ball to get it close to the hole. After hitting about a dozen of these shots, you should be able to get up and down about 25% of the time out of the trap. And that's a low figure for really unsuccessful athletes. With some practice, you can double that percentage.

There is one exception I must mention. There are many different kinds of sand. For example, masonry sand is not the same as good sand trap sand. But some golf course superintendents don't know this. So, if your course has bad sand, really fluffy, with no body, this shot will be more difficult. Try to practice this shot after a rainstorm, when the sand is more compacted. Then you'll see what I mean.

But if your course has good sand, this shot is simple and easy.

The keys are:
- Dig into the sand with your feet until you are down to solid footing.
- Think of the bounce as the face of the club and establish this by laying the club face open (flat).
- Hit the sand about 1 inch behind the ball taking a shallow divot about the size of a dollar bill.
- Follow through.

Of course, all the swing tips I've given you 'til now are still in play. Head still, magic move, proper weight transfer, right elbow in. You will want to pick the club up a little quicker than you do with a normal fairway shot—-not the usual low backswing. And I recommend a ¾ backswing (about 1:30 or 2:00 o'clock). You're not trying to hit the ball 300 yards.

If you get real good at this shot, you'll be able to put backspin on the ball. But don't worry if you can't, it isn't important. Just learn to do what you can with this shot. It's effective even without backspin. (One way to help effect the backspin is to open your stance a little, and cut across the ball giving it more English, and not digging as deeply into the sand)

One last tip. Digging in with your feet accomplishes two things:
1. It establishes a solid footing for you.
2. It gives you information of the depth of the sand in the trap. For example, since you are trying to take a divot 1 inch under the ball, it is a good thing to know if the sand is at least an inch deep!

The 18th hole of the course I used to play in Phoenix was a long par 4, with a pond on the left of the green, and a sand trap on the right. In order to avoid the water, I used to aim for the trap. Better to miss right (the trap, which I could play out of without penalty) than left (the water, which I could not play from at all.) Because of my good sand game, I usually expected to par this hole.

FAIRWAY SAND SHOTS: These are a little bit more difficult than greenside sand shots, because you actually have to hit the ball.

Hitting the ball out of a fairway bunker requires special consideration.

No matter how far you are from the green, your first challenge is to get the ball out of the trap and back into play. So, if you are 200 yards from the green, and have a lip 5 feet high in front of you, forget the 200 yards, and get the ball up and out of the trap. If that means 8 iron, use 8 iron. Believe me, a 3 iron won't get you on the green if it doesn't get high enough soon enough to clear that lip!

If you don't have lip problems, then it's no sweat. Take one club longer than you would use from whatever distance you have to hit, dig in to a solid footing, and hit the ball. In this case, you must hit the ball cleanly, taking a sand divot only after hitting the ball. Play the shot exactly as you would hitting off hard pan…hit the ball cleanly with a descending blow, then hit down into the sand and follow through. And, with this shot, a short backswing is a must. Take a practice swing before going into the trap to put the right moves into your computer-brain.

Even we "sweepers" take a divot on this shot, but only after we have hit the ball cleanly.

You can use irons or woods with this shot, whatever you're comfortable swinging. For longer irons and for woods, I'd recommend choking down an inch or so on the grip of the club for a little more control, and, again, shorten your backswing a bit, and swing solidly, with good rhythm.

If you are uncomfortable with this shot, take a shorter club and hit the ball part-way to the green. Then hit a shorter, easier, hundred yard or so shot on to the green. Remember, we are trying to break 90, so take the easiest shot for you to control, get on the green with a minimum of difficulty, and two putts.

LONG GREENSIDE SAND SHOTS: On the other hand, most good golfers will tell you that one of the toughest shots of all, is the greenside sand shot from longer than 10 or 20 yards. Some greenside traps stretch 50 yards from the green, or farther. And if you are farther away than your normal sand shot goes, you've got a very difficult shot.

Some recommend taking a 9 iron, and hitting the ball as if you were closer to the hole and were using a sand wedge, only with the face of the club more up-right. The more upright loft will send the ball lower and farther. I've seen this work.

Others recommend using the 9 iron and hitting the ball like a pitch shot off of hard pan. Pick it clean, then take a divot, making sure you hit the ball hard enough to go as far as you want it to.

I've tried both methods, had both work, and had both fail. Personally, I prefer the "hardpan pick" method. At least I am hitting the ball, and hard enough to get to the target. But here, a lot depends on the consistency of the sand, and your lie, and any hazards beyond your target.

After you become adept at hitting greenside trap shots, try these two solutions and see which works best for you.

FRIED EGG SAND SHOTS: Use your sand wedge, but hold the blade in a more upright position, and hit the shot like a greenside sand shot, but swing harder. And don't expect the same accuracy.

SAND SHOTS IN SOFT SAND, WITH UPHILL LIE, CLOSE TO THE LIP, AND CLOSE TO THE GREEN: These lies are often partially (and sometimes completely) buried. Be careful with this shot. DO NOT HIT THE BALL! You'll drive it deeper into the sand. Hit behind the ball, and scoop the sand up onto the green. This is not a finesse shot or a shot with any accuracy. Here, all you can do, is try to get onto the green and only lose one shot.

SAND SHOTS WHERE YOU HAVE NO SHOT, THE BACK OR FRONT OF YOUR BALL IS UP AGAINST THE LIP OF THE TRAP, AND YOU HAVE NO SHOT AT ALL: Here, you have no choice. There is no way you can advance the ball toward the flagstick or even the green. Study the situation, checking for a target to the right or left that will put you in the best position to get on the green and close to the hole with your next shot. Then, just try to get out of the trap and to that spot.

GREENSIDE SAND SHOTS WHERE THE TRAP HAS NO LIP, AND THE SAND IS FIRM. You may find this situation on some golf courses. And it's legal to putt the ball onto the green.

SIDEHILL LIES: Many fairways have lies that are not level. When you take your stance, the ball is above or below your feet. Here is the solution to these sidehill lies.

<u>Ball above your feet</u>: Take a couple of practice swings. You'll notice that you have a tendency to hit behind the ball. So, you have to make 2 adjustments:

- Play the ball farther back in your stance.
- Since the ball will be struck sooner than usual, adjust the timing of your wrist action, so that you'll be square at impact.

Main swing thoughts:

- You **must** keep your head still
- You'll have a tendency stay back on your back foot, and not transfer your weight. Be sure to get your weight off that back foot.

Finally, there is a tendency to pull the ball left. Guard against that.

<u>Ball below your feet</u>: This shot is more difficult for me than ball above my feet. Again, take a practice swing and see where the club head hits the ground… probably forward of normal. With this shot, there is a very strong tendency to lift your head, both on the backswing, and as you swing through the ball. Be very careful not to move your head.

When you take your stance, bend your knees. If you lean too far over to get to the ball, you'll fall down the hill, so your swing will be more upright than normal. And, in order not to have a big gap between the hill and the toe of your club, move your hands away from your body a bit.

With this shot, the tendency is to fade or slice the ball. Guard against that by timing your hands and hitting through the ball with strong wrist action.

When hitting both of these shots, remember the basics, and do not try anything cute. Just hit the ball smoothly, with good rhythm. Don't be fancy or try to overachieve by hitting an impossible shot.

UPHILL LIES: There is a lot of bad information out there about hitting off uphill lies.

The first thing I would recommend is for you to draw a clubhead circle, and draw a line under the circle representing the ground on an angle. Notice that the circle touches the ground uphill of the absolute bottom of the circle. This shows you graphically, that when hitting uphill, play the ball forward (uphill) in your stance, and the reverse is true for downhill shots.

Again, take a practice swing, watching where your club head hits the ground. Most pros recommend adjusting your shoulders parallel to the hill, and swinging "uphill" at the ball. That's all right, but don't get carried away with adjusting your shoulders. If your downhill shoulder is too low, you'll have a tendency to hit way behind (downhill of) the ball

I give in a little to the shoulder adjustment, but I try to keep my backswing almost the same as with a level lie. I drop it a little, but not too much. I find that, with uphill lies, I take a longer club, and hit the ball hard, trying almost to drive the ball into the hillside. I always take a divot on this shot, after I've hit the ball. The uphill lie adds loft to the club and drives the ball up the hill.

Expect the ball to fly higher than normal, and to lose distance, of course. Sometimes, you need a club 3 or 4 numbers longer than you would normally hit for that distance. Again, be smooth. Don't swing too hard. Make sure you make good contact.

Finally, with this shot there is a big tendency to pull the ball. After all, the ball is farther forward than normal, and by the time your club head gets to it, you'll have your wrists closed, and be swinging around, outside to inside. Make the instinctive adjustment, and be sure your timing is adjusted to the ball position, and that you are still swinging downline toward your target when you get to the ball.

DOWNHILL LIES: The circle and uphill lie diagram works the same for downhill lies, only reversed. The circle hits the ground uphill (or behind) the bottom of the circle. So what will happen, is that your club head will hit the ground sooner, closer to your back foot.

There are several adjustments you must make.

Firstly, you will have difficulty completing your full backswing, especially on severe downhill lies. Even tilting your shoulders down the hill, your uphill leg and upper body will interfere with your making the back-swing turn. So adjust with a shorter backswing.

Secondly, getting to the ball sooner, means that you will still be swinging inside-out more than with your normal timing, so, expect to hit the ball to the right, and adjust, both your alignment and your wrist-timing to make sure the ball is going along the desired line.

Finally, the angle of the hill plus the angle of the clubface, combine to give you a really good chance of blading the ball (cutting the ball with the leading edge of the clubface). You need a more upright club-face, so you will have a better chance of actually hitting the ball with the face of the club. You can see what I mean by taking a wedge to a downhill lie, and addressing a ball. What you get is a great chance to blade the ball. Be smart! Use a less lofted club, and swing easier.

Going downhill, you'll get better roll and more distance with your club, so adjust for that eventuality.

HITTING HIGH, OVER AN OBSTACLE: Play the ball forward in your stance, pick your club head up quicker than on a normal shot, with a more upright swing, and hit DOWN on the ball. Of course, common sense will tell you, use the high lofted club necessary to do the job.

HITTING LOW, UNDER AN OBSTACLE: Play the ball back in your stance, use a low lofted, 2, 3, or 4 iron. Use a flatter swing, and use a club that is more than enough to go the distance you want to hit. Hit the shot softly. Tiger hits a 1 iron hard, and it soars up in the sky. But if you hit the ball softly, it stays low to the ground.

HITTING WITH A SHORT BACKSWING (UNDER, OR UP AGAINST A TREE): If your ball comes to rest in a place where you have a restricted backswing, you must accept that you'll have very few options. Often, you are farther away from the green than you can reach with a restricted swing, so you must adjust.

Firstly, chose a club with the thought of getting a clear shot. If your only problem is distance and direction, use a club that is sure to keep the ball low, under any hazard. Practice your shortened backswing. When you hit the ball, choke down on the club, swing flat, and play the ball back in your stance, near the back foot, because there will be almost no weight transfer with this shot, and your clubhead will hit the ground sooner than expected. The ball should come out low, and get a lot of roll, because you'll impart more than the usual topspin.

CHAPTER 8: HOW TO THINK ON A GOLF COURSE!!!

No high handicapper knows how to think on a golf course, or he wouldn't be a high handicapper.

Let me give you a graphic example of not thinking on a golf course. I'm standing on the 5th tee with a 62 year old man who has a withered left arm and has just played 4 holes with a bogey, 2 doubles and a triple. I'll bet you can guess what he is saying.

"I'll have to par in from here."

Par is for young healthy pros. He's not young, healthy, or a pro!!! Is he using his brain??? HELL NO!

Check your foursome the next time you're on the course on a steaming hot sunny day. How many are looking for shade, and how many are just standing in the sun waiting for their next shot? You'll see I'm right. Most golfers don't use their brains on a golf course!

Most of you 100 plus scorers could be shooting in the 90's or better if only you knew the strategy of how to beat the course and how to use your intelligence to make the game easier; to keep you out of trouble; and to put you into position to cut useless, stupid strokes off your score card. It is disheartening to watch a person who hits the ball well enough to be scoring in the 80's or 90's, but who doesn't even try to think about how to save 20 wasted strokes a round.

Here are some of the thoughts I have already mentioned:
- You don't work at golf like a pro. Don't expect to hit shots like a pro.
- Practice your short game, pitching, chipping, and putting once in a while at home, on a carpet or in your backyard.
- No more than two putts per green, and don't try to sink any putt over 6 feet…just try to get it close to the hole for a tap-in.
- Par is for pros. If your goal is bogey golf, you can take easier, safer shots, and easily reach your goal of breaking 90.
- Always look for the easy, safe shot!

Let's start before the first tee. (There's a reason why the best golfers in your club will be found on the practice tee half an hour before they tee off.)

To prove what I'm about to say, the next time you play, see if you don't get more "into the swing" of the game after three or four holes of play. That comfort would start on the first tee if you had warmed up on the practice tee.

Before you play, spend 15 or 20 minutes on the practice tee. Loosen up. Starting with the easy 9 irons and 7 irons, work your way up through the mid-irons and hybrids. Then hit a few fairway woods and finally, a few drives. Save 6 or 8 balls to hit pitch shots at a target 30 or 40 yards away…even if that target is only a ball someone mis-hit earlier. This practice is for "loosening up", and adjusting your timing, and for entering information into your computer brain, not for improving your swing.

Go to the putting green and practice a few chips onto the green, then putts. Practice the 25 footers to get the feel of the speed of the green. Then hit several putts from inside 6 feet into the hole. You should spend a minimum of 30 minutes before every round warming up as described.

On the first tee, it is more important to hit the fairway 210-225 yards out, than to lose the ball in the woods 300 yards out. Swing within yourself.

Do not tee the ball up in the middle of the tee box and aim for the middle of the fairway. If you routinely slice the ball, expect to slice your drive, and allow for the slice. A good friend of mine used to have a terrible slice which he couldn't control. His solution was to tee the ball at the very right corner of the tee box, and aim diagonally across to a spot down the left side of the fairway.

His reasoning was, if he teed the ball in the middle and aimed for the middle, his slice had only half a fairway to work with. Aiming diagonally across the fairway gave him the entire width of the fairway to absorb his slice and keep him in play. And if his shot accidentally went straight, or a little left, there was some room for that, too.

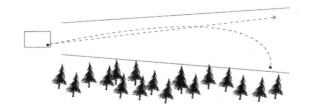

CAPTION: Slicers, tee right and aim left. Use the entire width of the fairway to absorb your slice.

Of course, the opposite strategy is for the hookers. Tee left and aim right.

By the way, by correcting his shoulders at address, and the timing of his wrists, I was able to correct my friend's slice in two minutes.

Jack Nicklaus used to hit a slight fade. He didn't aim for the flag. He aimed a little left of the flag, and let his fade move the ball toward the flagstick. If you hit a slice, don't aim for the target. Aim left of the target, and let the slice carry you to the target.

Remember, on a par 4, your goal is three shots to the green and two putts. If that hole is under 400 yards long, a 225 yard drive puts you within 175 yards of the green. Two easy shots of about 100 yards each, (A 145 yard seven iron and a 30 yard pitch, for example.) will put you on the green from there. Then two-putt for your bogey 5. (And, by the way, if you're not breaking 100, you should be playing very few par 4 holes over 400 yards!)

If you have woods or sand traps or water, try to avoid them. If water is on the right, aim left. If a trap sits in front of the green, try to avoid it by taking another route. Go around it. Or lay up short of it, and hit an easy wedge over it onto the green.

Learn to take what the course gives you. Don't fight the course, you'll lose. If there is a hazard you are not positive you can clear on the fly, lay up short of it and hit the sure short shot over it. Give up one shot in order to save two or three. On those par 4's you are allowed to miss a shot and still score your 5.

Remember, 5 is par for you. Relax and play for the smart 5, rather than stressing and praying for a miracle that isn't going to happen. Play 2 easy short shots, staying away from woods, water, sand, and even rough, instead of trying one long shot which gives you problems and wastes shots. A sure 5 is better than a probable 6 or 7 from mis-hitting a long shot into trouble; especially when two short shots are almost certain success.

What is easier for you to hit well? A 2 or 3 iron, or a 7 or 8 iron. The seven and 8 have shorter shafts, higher lofts, and you can hit them surer and straighter. The difference between a 3 iron and an 8 iron is only 50 or 60 yards. If you are 200 yards from a green protected by hazards, don't try the 2 iron, play a 5 or 6 iron, then you only have an easy pitch to the green.

On the other hand, if there is no trouble between you and the green, by all means, go for it. But pick your spots. Figure in advance how you'll play each hole, taking advantage of the easy holes, and playing cautiously on the water holes and holes with narrow fairways and lots of sand.

There is no law that says you must use a driver on every tee. If your average drive goes 225, and there is a creek 200 yards out, take a 4 iron and lay up. Two more short, easy shots will get you on any par 4 from wherever you hit that 4 iron, even if you're like me, old and sick and weak and can only hit that 4 iron 140 yards.

If there is a dogleg that your driver will drive you through, hit a more appropriate, shorter club. If the landing area for your driver is narrow, with hazards right and left, lay up with a shorter club and take the easy, safe shot. **That's what the pros do!**

What I'm saying is that golf is a game dedicated to the **POWER OF NEGATIVE THINKING**. Ask yourself, "What's the worst thing that can happen to me here?" **THEN AVOID THAT!**

If your ball goes into the woods, don't try for that impossible shot between two trees 18 inches apart. **You have just missed a fairway 50 yards wide!** Look for the easiest, surest, biggest opening to the fairway, even if you have to hit it backwards! Then hit the ball back into play in the fairway!

But smarter still, don't hit it into the woods in the first place. Don't try to cut that dogleg with a perfect, 100 to 1 shot. Play around the dogleg in two easy shots. That's better than 1—into the woods: 2—out of the woods; 3—hit to where you should have been in two...and that's not counting the other shots trying to get out of the woods through little openings, or the 2 shot penalty for lost balls...or the **cost** of the lost balls.

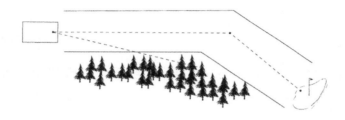

CAPTION: Take the safe shot around the trees. Don't gamble on cutting the dogleg and losing strokes in the woods.

If the left side of the fairway is lined with traps, or has a stream running all the way down it, play the right side of the fairway! If you're not sure you can play the right side of the fairway, use a shorter club you are sure will work.

Think! Fight Back! Don't give in to your opponent, the golf course. You can't beat it, but you can keep it from battering you silly.

Always take the easy way out. Remember, you have an extra stroke on every hole. Use those strokes, and even if in the beginning, you have to use another, extra shot...90 + 9 additional extra shots still breaks 100!

I can't overemphasize the short game. When you are 2 putting every green, when you are hitting those chip shots and pitch shots up close to the pin for 1 putt greens, it really doesn't matter how you hit your long shots. Your best scoring days will be when you hit the long ball ok, but chip and putt like a genius...like a Tiger!! (Seriously, do you remember Tiger's drives, or his chips and putts?)

Another big mistake to overcome. Make sure you are aiming where you think you are aiming. On **<u>every shot</u>**, my pre-shot routine sets me up on the line I want to hit the ball.

I stand behind my ball, and pick a **safe** target. Then I sight a line from that specific target back to my ball, paying particular attention to the last foot or so, of that line, the foot closest to my ball. I try to pick a mark, a divot, a leaf, a bare spot, something I can isolate on, on, or just off my line.

Then I walk up to my ball, and, putting my club behind the ball so that it is aimed over my spot, I take my stance. Then I settle in, guided in my set up by my club head. And, on my first waggle, I pass the club head in front of the ball, aiming it at my target, and sighting past it, down the line at my target, just to make sure I'm aiming where I **think** I'm aiming. If I'm not, I don't hit the ball until I'm aligned correctly.

Once I'm perfectly lined up, I **never move my feet.** That's why my ball always stays in play. Even when I miss the shot, and hit a worm-burner, I'm still advancing my ball on the right line toward my target.

The course I play right now has a par 3 hole which is lined with traps from the tee to the green, all the way down the right side of a very narrow fairway. The front of the green is 155 yards away, and doglegs back to the right, behind all the traps.

I told you, I'm old and sick and weak, and my driver only goes 175 yards...most of it roll. I don't have a club in my bag that will carry 155 yards in the air, much less stop on the green after that flight. So here's how I play this hole.

I tee the ball on the right side of the tee, and hit my 5 wood (my 150 yard club) at a spot on the left side of the fairway, in front of the green. Then I try to chip on and one-putt. I par this hole about 40 % of the time, because I stay out of the traps, and I can chip and putt well. And bogey is still 4! A good number when 5 is par on every hole.

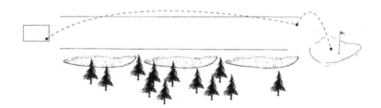

CAPTION My strategy for the long par 3 protected by sand traps which I can't carry in the air.

If you don't believe what I'm telling you in this chapter, I want you to try two things:

1. After your next round of golf, count all the wasted strokes hit from the woods. Count the penal-

ty strokes from lost balls and shots hit into the water. Count the extra strokes from the traps. Then subtract them from your score. I'll bet they bring you under 100.

2. Sometime when you're not playing for anything, on a par 4 hole, hit an easy drive with your 3 or 4 wood or even a hybrid. On your next shot, try an easy 5, 6, or 7 iron, leaving, probably, less than 50 yards to the green. Next, hit your easy short shot somewhere onto the green, then, finally, try to get down in 2 putts. You'll see how easy it really is!

Jack Nicklaus said, "My great shots are no better than the average duffer's great shots. But my bad shots are a lot better than that duffer's."

Remember, don't hit those really bad shots that get you into trouble from where there is no rescue. Remember the power of negative thinking...what's the worst thing that can happen? Then avoid that!!!

CHAPTER 9: TIPS & OTHER NONSENSE

- Unless you know, standing on the first tee, that your score will be better than 85, you should be playing the shortest tees allowed.
- After you've hit a really bad shot, slow down, take a deep breath, and calm down. Remember, two bad shots are worse than one bad shot.
- Go to your local pro shop and buy and read <u>The Rules of Golf.</u> It amazes me that people play golf, poker, and a lot of other games, and **don't even know the rules!** If you can imagine, Craig Stadler, a top touring pro, once was disqualified from the San Diego Open because he had to hit a shot from his knees, and to keep from getting grass stains on his pants, he laid a towel on the ground, then knelt on the towel…2 stroke penalty for "building a stance", and disqualification from the tournament for signing a scorecard which did not include the 2 penalty strokes.
- The wind exaggerates everything. Hitting into the wind makes a short shot shorter. Hitting into the wind bends a slice or a hook worse, just as a crosswind adds extra bend to hooks and slices. Wind even affects putts. But, like water, wind is not a difficult enemy to conquer. You know he will always act the

same way. Use the wind. Play **with** the wind. Do not fight the wind.

- It does no good to talk to the ball. The last thing they do before they ship them from the factory is cut the little ears off of them.
- Don't waste time and energy bending over to pull up some grass to throw to check the wind. Use your ears. Feel the wind on your face and ears to tell you which way the wind is blowing, and how hard. When you feel the wind on both ears, you're either facing into the wind or with it. Is the wind on your face?
- In 1958, Tommy Bolt won the U.S. Open. He had, he said, discovered a new secret, one which simplified his swing, and always put him in perfect position at the top of his backswing. It came to him, that it was not best for him to set his wrists at the top of his backswing, where he could not see them. Actually, it was better to set them early in the swing, when he could see his hands, and be sure that they were correct. This new idea gave him confidence in his swing, which carried through to his whole game, and he won the tournament.

Well, that's a good idea for us duffers, too, especially, if you have weak wrists; women, juniors, and many men, as well. Too many of us cock our wrists at the top of the backswing, then, because our wrists are weak, our hands spring back into a "casting" motion, and ruin our swing. If our hands are set before they reach the top, they will not "bounce" back, and we'll have a nice, smooth transition from backswing to throughswing.

- In keeping with Tommy Bolt's secret, you might want to try a forward press just prior to beginning your backswing. This is a little move you probably have seen some professionals do. Keeping the club head on the ground in the address position, they move their hands a little bit forward, beginning the wrist cock as a trigger to begin the backswing, thus cocking their wrists perfectly at the very beginning of the backswing.

- An easy bet to win...Have your opponent hit two shots every time, teeing off through putting out; then **you** pick the **worst** one for him to play on his next shot. I used to play this bet regularly with a 3 handicapper (I was a 6) and give him a stroke a hole. He never came close to beating me. I've heard that Jack Nicklaus estimated he couldn't break 85 playing that way.

- Practice stopping midway through your swing. It's hard to do, but, sometimes, halfway through a swing, you realize that something is not right...you've lost your balance, or bumped a divot on your backswing and thrown off your timing. If you can stop, and start your swing over, you'll eliminate an almost certain bad shot. There is no "balk" in golf.

- Never stand over your ball at address and say to yourself, "XXX is wrong, but on this swing I'll adjust." (XXX being wrong ball position, alignment, whatever.) Back away and start over.

- Always take a towel with you to the golf course, for two reasons: (1) to clean clubs, balls, and yourself, and (2) when you take more than one club from your bag, take the towel along. You may forget your wedge, but you won't forget your towel!

- Unless you are backed up on the golf course, allow faster players through if they wish. Always be courteous on the golf course.

- After you finish a hole, get off the green, into your cart, and get out of the way of the foursome following you. Don't waste time cleaning clubs, putting them into your bag, or writing your score. Do all that on the next tee. Get out of the way!

- And, after your round, don't stand on (or near) the 18th green adding up your score. Get out of the way!

- If you're lazy like I am, you don't have to use golf shoes with spikes. Back in the 80's and 90's, when courses began no longer allowing steel spikes, they sold "spikeless" shoes. I figure, if spikeless shoes were ok then, they're still ok. So, I use normal street shoes when I play golf, because I'm too lazy to change shoes in my car. But, choose your soles and heels carefully, don't slip all over the course in leather soles and heels...use rubber, even maybe, with ridges or some other gripping shape. Your shoe repairman has appropriate soles and heels for golf. (**DON'T USE FOOTBALL OR SOCCER CLEATS OR BASEBALL SPIKES!)**

- Before you give your shoes to a locker room attendant to clean and shine, check his other work. These days, with so few of them serving in the military, a lot of those guys never learned how to shine shoes. Many are so bad that they ruin a good shine, so badly it's tough to get a good shine back.

- I once joined a threesome of strangers on the first tee. On the second green, one of the men left his putt about a foot short, and I graciously, I thought, gave him the putt. "Hold on there!" one of the other men said, "We're playing for $20 a hole! I'll tell him when the putt is given!" Lesson learned.

- If you are playing with a beginner, young children, a wife just learning the game, make it fun. Play Captain's Choice. Everyone tees off on every hole. Then, pick the best shot, and everyone play from there. That way, no one is embarrassed, and you don't hold up the course. And if you have kids along, make it interesting for them. Let the kids drive the cart. I used to take my three nephews out to play captain's choice, let them take turns driving the cart (they sat in my lap in the driver's seat and I worked the pedals until they were big enough to work them.) Then we'd go to McDonalds for a lavish dinner, and then to a movie. We all loved it, and we got to spend quality time together.

- A swing thought to help you keep your head still...float on your knees. Keep your knees bent, and "float" on them, not raising your body up from your address position.

- There is a mathematical Rule of 9's. Add up the digits of a hole number, and they total the number of the hole in that nine. The 14th hole is the 5th hole of that nine...1 + 4 = 5. The 133rd hole would be the 7th hole of that nine. 3 + 3 + 1 =...you know.
- When you can afford them, new, professionally fitted clubs are terrific, and will really affect your game positively. I have a friend, John, who got fitted by a really good club fitter, and his game went from a 15 handicap to a 7 immediately. Mike Reid, a tour player, used to hit his drives 242, 243. Now, he's on the <u>Senior</u> Tour, and, with 21st Century clubs, his average drive is 276 yards. See what a difference clubs can make!
- Amateurs leave birdie putts short.
- Don't believe that old saw about hitting a new ball over water. Mr. Spalding thought up that idea, so he could sell more new balls.
- Never wash your ball prior to hitting over water. The ball might decide that it likes water, and dive into the pond.
- If you need to change your luck, wash your ball...ONCE! (Twice changes your luck right back.)
- If you lose a lot of balls, don't buy $4.00 Pro V1's. Buy the Spalding Top Flights, 15 to the box for $14.95. (It's called "Thinking".)

- **If you want scientific evidence of what you need to practice, rate all your shots on a scale of 1 to 5.**
  1 is a shot so good it saved a stroke.
  2 is a shot good enough to probably save you a stroke.
  3 is what you expected.
  4 probably will cost a stroke.
  5 surely will cost you a stroke.
  Average your drives, long shots, short shots, and putts separately.
  Practice everything averaging over 3. (Keep track on a score card.)
- A good way to keep track of your score. Instead of writing down how many strokes you hit on the hole, just write down how many you were over (or under) par...bogey is 1, double bogey is 2, birdie is 1 with a ring around it. At the end of the nine holes, add up the ones and twos, and add that to par.
- Two quick fixes when your timing and kinetic energy aren't working and you're not hitting the ball straight. (1) Try holding the club firmer with whichever hand is on the side the ball is leaking toward...fading too much, squeeze harder with your right hand (rightys). (2) Try that baseball swing you first used to adjust your timing...break your wrists sooner if fading, later if drawing.

Well, that's it. Before we part, let me tell you one last story.

One day, at a local public course, I met a man named King. He had a first name, but I don't remember it, I just called him "King". King had been a pro, but had got his amateur status back, and twice, he won the Columbia South Carolina City Championship. King was a very good golfer.

Anyway, we met up on the first tee, agreed to play together, and hit off. I hit my usual 225 yard drive right down the middle, and King hit his drive, easy and smooth, and, it looked like it was right down the middle, too.

We got to my ball, and I started looking around for King's ball, maybe even with mine, or maybe a little ahead. I didn't see it.

I asked, "Where's your ball?"

He said, "A little ahead."

Well, this was a par 5, so I hit my 3 wood, about 210 yards, which would put me, probably, 80 yards from the green. And we started walking, but I still didn't see King's ball.

Finally, about 200 yards from the green, we found it...right in the middle of the fairway. King had hit a 310 yard drive...this back in the 1960's when the longest drivers on Tour were averaging less than 280 yards off the tee!

I didn't believe it! He hadn't swung especially hard, he wasn't big and tall, or extra strong looking. I had never seen anyone hit a ball that far! For the next 4 holes, I tried to kill the ball, trying to keep up with King, which was far beyond the realm of possibility.

Finally, about halfway down the 5th fairway, after playing terribly, I came to my senses. I wasn't capable of playing King's game. I had to settle down and stick to MY game. Do what I do best.

From then on, playing within myself, I played King even. From the 6th through the 18th holes, we had the same total score.

That day I learned a valuable lesson. Do what I do, the way I do it. Don't worry about how the other guy plays, what club he's using, or how far he hits the ball. I'm OK playing my game. I know what I can do, and I can do it well. I can't beat him at HIS game, but maybe, playing MY game I can win.

Play within yourself always...you play YOUR game. Good Luck!